Weapo

Secrets of the
Karambit

David Seiwert

Copyright © 2016 David Seiwert
All rights reserved.

www.DavidSeiwert.com

www.DynamicFightingArt.com

www.DfaMediaProductions.com

ISBN-13: 978-1530527953
First Edition 2016
1st revision - April 2016

All rights reserved. No part of this publication may be reproduced, distributed or transmitted in any form, including photocopying or other electronic or mechanical methods without prior permission of the author.

Thank you for respecting the hard work of the writer and those involved in the making of this book.

DEDICATION

To all of my instructors over these many years for their help and patience in guiding me along my path, to my students who I continue to learn from and all martial artists who have an open mind and truly want to learn.

And a special thanks to my wife for putting up with me for all of these years.

DISCLAIMER

Please note that the publisher, the author, or anyone appearing in this instructional book is Not Responsible in any manner whatsoever for any injury which may occur by reading and/or following the instructions herein. When training you should wear safety glasses and ALWAYS use a practice training karambit.

This book is for informational purposes only.

It is essential that before following any of the activities, physical or otherwise, herein described, the reader or readers should first consult his or her physician for advice on whether or not the reader or readers should embark on the physical activity described herein. Since the physical activities described herein may be too sophisticated in nature, it is essential that a physician be consulted.

It is also advised to check with your local law enforcement for guidance on self-defense. Use the minimal force necessary to overcome an attacker.

ACKNOWLEDGMENTS

I would like to thank the following individuals, for without their contributions and support this book would not have been written:

Joe Hinnenkamp, Brandon Jones, Gene Knuff, Trevor Lynch, Bill Steelman, Dave Thompson, Sean Westrich, Don Wong for their help demonstrating the techniques.

My wife Thana and Don Wong for their great photography work.

Thank you to my Beta readers Chris Lagdameo and Bill Steelman.

Other books by the author:
KunTao - The esoteric martial art of Southeast Asia

Cover design by DFA Media Productions

Published by DFA Media Productions

CONTENTS

Part 1 - What is a Karambit?

1. History
2. Parts of the Karambit
3. Alloys
4. Design
5. Grips
6. Deployment
7. Types of Karambits

Part 2 - Karambit Basics

8. Being Responsible
9. Pre-empting an Attack
10. Karambit Striking Pattern
11. Blocking
12. Entries
13. Hand Grabs
14. Footwork
15. Solo Training
16. Training Drills
17. Impact Strikes
18. Body Manipulations

19 Street Defense
20 Zombie Apocalypse
21 Joint Locking
22 Unarmed vs. Karambit
23 Karambit vs. Straight Blade
24 Karambit vs. Gun
   Final Thoughts
   Appendices
   References

FOREWARD

The karambit has become extremely popular in recent years, spread by practitioners of Southeast Asian martial arts such as Silat, KunTao and the Filipino arts of Kali and Escrima, but there seems to be a scarcity of information on the subject outside of these arts.

More and more martial arts styles as well as law enforcement (LEO) and the military are looking into the usefulness of this ancient Indonesian weapon, but with a dearth of teaching material and or instructors out there, they are forced to learn on their own or try to find someone who is at least familiar with this unique weapon.

It is my hope that this book will help everyone interested in learning the karambit to gain a better understanding of this fascinating utility tool and fighting implement.

David Seiwert

To view video clips of some of the following drills and techniques go to:

https://goo.gl/YEuuQR

Part 1 - What is a Karambit?

Chapter 1

History

The karambit is a small handheld, curved knife resembling a tiger's claw that was initially found in Southeast Asia.

Typically called kErambit in its native Malay region (southern Myanmar, Malaysia, Indonesia, Singapore, Brunei and southern Thailand, it is referred to as the kArambit in the Philippines and in most Western countries.

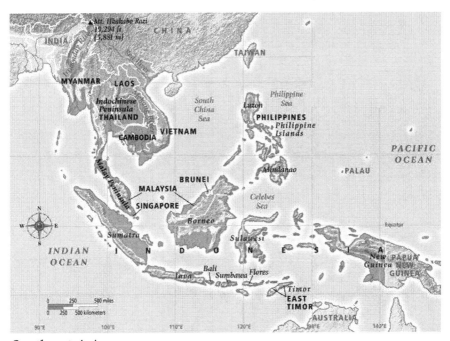

Southeast Asia

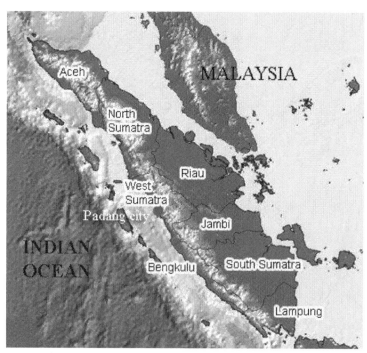

West Sumatra

The karambit is believed to have originated around the 11th century CE (Common Era or 11 AD) among the Minangkabau people who are an indigenous ethnic group of West Sumatra, Indonesia. According to folklore, the karambit was inspired by the claws of the larger species of cats such as the tiger which are found throughout Southeast Asia.

People of Minangkabau playing Silek

As with many of your traditional weapons, it was primarily used as an agricultural implement designed for raking roots, gather threshing and planting rice just as the Japanese nunchuck was originally a farming instrument used for flailing rice.

The ancient Sunda people believed that when a king died, his spirit was transported into the jungles and became the spirit of the tiger. They were awestruck by the power and beauty of the tiger (pak macan, pamacan), and believed that its claws would give them special powers. They would often adorn themselves with necklaces made of actual tiger claws and this eventually led to the creation of a blade which mimicked the tiger's claw, the Kuku Macan.

Kuku Macan   Lawi Ayam or 'Cocks Tail Feather'

The kuku macan, comes from Sumatra, Indonesia and means 'claw of tiger'. The kuku macan is a larger version of a knife called Lawi Ayam or 'cock's tail feather', both of which are related to the karambit.

It was said that centuries ago the blade edge of the kuku macan was treated with toxins from various species of poisonous frogs, snakes, spiders and scorpions to quickly kill the opponent from even the smallest cut, adding to the mystique of the weapon.

There are many ancient designs of knife with a blade shape similar to the karambit such as the Kuku Macan, Janbiya, Khanjar and Kubikiri Tanto however, the latter were designed as weapons and not as farming implements or utility knives as was the karambit.

One should also note that these blades don't have the familiar "finger ring" that makes the karambit unique.

Janbiya

Janbiya, is the Arabic expression for a dagger or knife, however it is used to define a particular type of blade with a short curved blade mostly associated with the people of western Saudi Arabia, and Yemen.

The word janibya is derived from the Arabic word janb which means 'side' because it is typically worn on the side of the individual's body.

Khanjar is the term used for the janibya in eastern Saudi Arabia, the United Arab Emirates, Oman, as well as in Syria and Iraq.

The Kubikiri Tanto comes from Japan and translates as 'head cutter' in Japanese the kubikiri was used to remove the heads of dead enemy soldiers as trophies of battle.

Kubikiri Tanto

*****

Culturally the karambit was looked down upon by the military in Indonesia because it was known as a weapon of farmers and peasants.

However, the renowned Bugis warriors in the South Sulawesi province of Indonesia were known to embrace the use of the karambit. The Bugis had a reputation as fierce and skilled warriors who helped to establish the Buginese Kingdom of the pre-colonial era.

The Bugis realized that the curved shape of the blade made it a formidable weapon and when holding the karambit in the reverse position (blade point facing downward) the user is able to develop tremendous force by the twisting of the waist allowing the wielder to drive the blade into and through the attacker.

When people started using it more as a weapon, the blade became longer and more curved to maximize the cutting potential such as with the Karambit Besar.

The Karambit Besar being much longer was able to make deeper cuts allowing soldiers to literally eviscerate the enemies by disemboweling them.

Karambit Besar

According to European accounts the Indonesian soldiers were armed with a kris strapped to their waist or back and a spear in their hands, the karambit was seen as a last resort or back-up when the fighter's other weaponry was lost in battle much like the Wakazashi and Katana. While it is an excellent weapon for slashing, it is not able to penetrate the body deep enough to be considered a killing weapon.

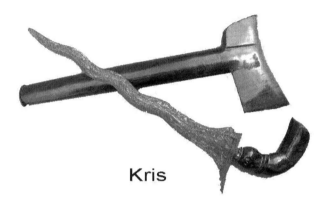

Kris

*****

The Karambit was also popular among the Indonesian women of that time who would tie the weapon into their hair or hide it in the folds of their sarong to be used in emergency situations.

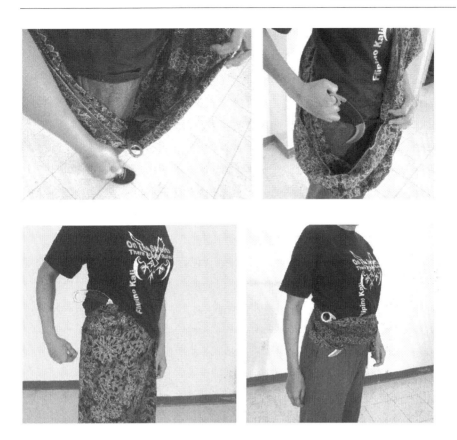

In time, the karambit was eventually adopted into Pencak Silat (also spelled Pentjak Silat), the indigenous and deadly close-combat fighting art of Indonesia and is recognized as one of the main weapons of the art.

Though even today among modern silat practitioners the karambit is still regarded as a feminine weapon much as the dart or a hand held fan in Chinese martial arts and the ko-naginata in the Japanese arts.

This idea of a smaller or exclusively "female" weapon is not really that unusual, and even today many modern day women may carry mace, a small knife or a gun (.22, .32, .380 calibers) for protection.

As a result of Indonesia's close contact and thriving commerce trade with neighboring countries, the karambit was eventually spread throughout Southeast Asia to what are now Cambodia, Laos, Malaysia, Myanmar, Thailand and the Philippines.

The karambit made its way into western culture during the last 30-40 yrs, being introduced by practitioners of Southeast Asian martial arts, most notably Silat, KunTao and Filipino Kali. Although there are many different sizes of the karambit, in general the entire span of the karambit ranges anywhere from roughly 6" - 12" (15 - 30cm) in length though they can also be smaller or larger than this.

Due to the current popularity of the karambit, many other martial arts systems as well as the police and military are now adopting it, and adding the karambit into their systems or exploring ways to defend against the weapon.

If you really want to learn the intricacies of the karambit, then it is best for you to find someone experienced in the martial arts of Southeast Asia.

Chapter 2

Parts of the Karambit

While styles, features and designs of the karambit are constantly changing there are core features that all modern blades should have in order to be identified as a karambit.

They include:
1) Point
2) Curved Blade - this could be a long or short blade with varying degrees of curvature, this is one of the main features that designate it as a karambit and allow for the hooking, tearing, and slicing performance of this blade.
3) Inside Edge
4) Outside Edge - a sharpened edge on the outside of the blade is usually only found on fixed blades. You will typically not find a folder that is double edged unless it was modified by the owner.
5) Ergonomic Handle
6) Retention or Safety Ring - not all of the original designs had this ring, but in contemporary times 90% of karambits possess the safety ring. This is the feature that sets the karambit apart from other knives.

The parts listed above are requirements that classify it as a karambit but in addition, most will also have:
7) Spine
8) Shaft/Tang

9) Thumb Rise
10) Front Brake
11) Rear Brake

These 11 parts are the elements that make up the bulk of karambits in use today. The curved blade and the retention ring are, of course, what make the karambit most easily identifiable and a coveted implement for martial arts training or for EDC (every day carry).

The retention ring promotes a quick extraction of the blade during deployment (by slipping the index finger through the ring) and ensures that the knife is ideally positioned in the user's hand and ready for engagement while the curved blade allows for ease of use and makes the application of this unique and exceptional tool seem effortless.

Chapter 3

Alloys

Now if we take a closer look at the karambit, and specifically into the types of base metals used to make this unique and evolutionary piece of history we find an intriguing account of blade forging and alloy evolution.

Up until the 11th century BCE (Before Common Era or 11 BC), metal implements were predominantly made of iron or bronze, but during that century it was discovered that iron could be greatly improved upon by adding carbon to the mix.

Pure iron, also known as "wrought iron" is not good for knife making because it is very soft and very brittle, but when a certain amount of carbon is added to the Iron it becomes much stronger and much tougher.

When iron is reheated in a furnace with charcoal (which contains carbon), some of the carbon is transferred to the iron. This process of adding carbon to the iron significantly hardens the metal. The process is further enhanced by rapidly cooling the metal, usually by quenching (thrusting the blade into water).

The new material (steel) can be formed (or 'wrought') just like the softer iron, and it is capable of being honed to a finer sharper edge. From the 11th century forward, the Iron Age was born and steel replaced bronze weapons in the Middle East.

Today all 'live' (edged) blades are of course made from steel, (with a few variations) but there are many types and grades available depending on what the user wants. A quick overview of the subject will be given here.

According to the American Iron & Steel Institute (AISI), Steel can be categorized into four basic groups (CAST) based on the chemical compositions:

Carbon Steel
Alloy Steel
Stainless Steel
Tool Steel

Most knives are made from tool grade steel but even within this category there are still many types, varieties and characteristics to choose from.

Basic steel is a combination of iron and carbon and over the years it was found that by adding different elements you could change the properties such as toughness or hardness.

Components such as chromium, nickel, tungsten, molybdenum, cobalt and vanadium can be added in varying quantities to increase heat resistance and durability, depending on the type of knife that you are looking to manufacture.

This can be a double edged sword though (no pun intended), for example if you harden the steel, it will hold a better edge, but you make it more brittle and susceptible to breaking. Let's take a quick look at the basic elements and their uses.

Carbon - This ingredient is essential to steel's creation; all steel will have some amount of carbon. It is the most important hardening element, but as it is added it can reduce the toughness of the material.
Chromium - Combats corrosion. Stainless steel knives contain chromium and this will also increase the strength of a knife.
Cobalt - Strengthens the blade.
Copper - Combats corrosion.
Manganese - Hardens the blade, but if added in high quantities it can increase brittleness.
Molybdenum - Maintains the steel's strength at high temperatures.
Nickel - Adds toughness.
Phosphorus - Improves strength.
Silicon - Increases strength and also will remove oxygen from the metal while it is being formed.
Sulfur - Makes it easier to machine, but decreases toughness.
Tungsten - Increases wear resistance.
Vanadium - Increases wear resistance and makes the blade harder.

Now we'll run through a brief summary of the types of steel most commonly used in knife forging.

The 10XX Series (plain carbon steel):

1045-1095 - any grade of steel within this range can also be used for knives, it's low cost, tough, holds a good edge and has been in use since WWII.

1050 - is commonly used for making swords.

1095 - is the most common type of 10XX steel used for knife blades.

The 400 Series (stainless):

410 stainless - Good for handles and liners, but not for blades

420 stainless - This steel is very soft, and doesn't hold an edge well, but it is good for making liner locks. It is low quality, low cost material and many inexpensive knives tend to be made of this material. However, 420 stainless steel is extremely rust resistant and is great for diving knives because of their constant contact with saltwater.

440 Stainless Steel - There are three different types of 440 steel.

440A Steel - This is a low cost stainless steel and is the most rust resistant of the 440 series.

440B Steel - Similar to 440A but has a higher carbon content. Makes a medium quality blade.

440C Steel - Considered a high end stainless steel and is the most common type used in making high quality knives.

5160 Steel - Is a common spring steel, and an excellent steel for swords, or any other blade that will have to take some battering.

52100 Steel - This steel is harder than many others, and holds an edge well. It is often for making hunting knives.

154 CM Steel - This is considered by many to be super-steel and has great corrosion resistance and good edge holding power. If you are looking for the best quality blade out there, then this is probably what you want.

ATS 34 Steel - This is very tough steel. And similar to 154 CM, it is also categorized as a super-steel and used for high end custom knives.

We can't end this section without talking about Damascus Steel which has made a resurgence in recent years.

Damascus steel was given that name because the first time the Europeans encountered this type of steel was during the Crusades in the 11th century CE, around the city of Damascus, Syria.

The reputation and history of Damascus steel has given rise to many legends, such as the ability to cut through a sword or rifle barrel, being able to cut a hair falling across the blade or splitting a feather in midair.

Damascus Steel

Damascus steel was originally created from 'wootz' steel which was developed in southern India around 1500 BCE and was the most advanced material known for 2 millennia (two thousand years). Damascus steel is easily recognizable by its distinctive 'flowing water' wave pattern on the blades.

Damascus steel was made by alternating two or more sheets of high and low carbon steel and folding them together multiple times. After the different layers of steel are folded together, the steel is acid etched, causing the color contrast and patterns on the blade to emerge revealing the flowing pattern of the folded layers of steel.

In the Middle East this type of steel was made for thousands of years, but eventually because of the secrecy among forgers and the development of new types of materials, the precise knowledge of how to create this metal was lost some time around the 17th century.

As a result the type of Damascus steel made today is not produced in the same manner as it was in ancient times and the 'water' pattern is actually made by pressing together multiple sheets of steel with a 40 ton press and then using acid etching to reproduce the look of ancient Damascus steel.

*****

So by this point you are probably wondering, "With so many types how do I know which is best"? Of course, this is subjective and is dependent on the design and purpose of the knife as well as the budget of the buyer.

Now there is a lot more about steel that we could go into, but since this is a book about karambits and not classifications of steel or knife making, we'll move on.

One final note, there is also a plethora of materials such as aluminum, high density plastics and wood that are used for making training blades so that you can safely train with your karambit.

NOTES

Chapter 4

Design

The design of a karambit blade varies slightly according to its geographic origin, generally the blades of Indonesia are more likely to be longer and not as curved, while those found in the Philippines and the west are smaller, shorter and they have a more pronounced curvature of the blade. This allows for the karambit to be used in a straight line thrust or punching type fashion as well as slashing attacks.

Philippine Style

Indonesian Style

There are many regional variants of the karambit, and the length of the blade may vary from one village blacksmith to the next, and even some karambits having two blades, one on either side of the handle.

In addition to the curved blade and handle the karambit is best known for the safety or retention ring at the end of the handle. While this is part of the original design for most karambits it is not a requirement and not all of them have one.

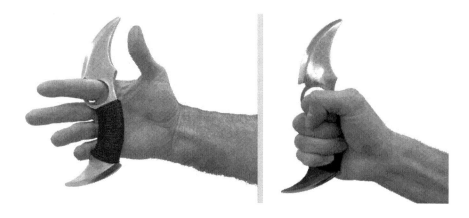

The original intent of the ring was to keep the blade from slipping from the user's hand while being used as a utility tool for cutting, digging or scraping. Since it was used in all kinds of conditions and environment, it would end up getting wet or covered in dirt or mud making the karambit slippery and difficult to hold.

With the retention ring the user can be assured that he will maintain possession of the karambit in any position even if he were to lose his footing.

In combat, placing the finger through the ring gives you a very secure grip and makes the karambit virtually impossible to lose or disarm because the karambit is secured by the design of the blade and not solely by the user's strength.

It also promotes a quick draw and solid deployment while ensuring that the knife is optimally positioned for use without requiring the user to ever take their eyes off the job at hand.

*****

When people see the karambit for the first time they are captivated by its design and it is rare to find a knife that excites the blade fancier more than the karambit. The karambits distinctive shape and appearance is what initially intrigues people and attracts them to the blade, but they soon learn that the karambits design is not only fascinating to look at but extremely functional as well.

One of the foremost advantages of the karambit is its compact size and the ability for concealment. When the blade is deployed in close combat situations and combined with the element of surprise, the karambit is virtually unstoppable even in the hands of a novice.

Despite the fact that the karambit can be intimidating in appearance, it is extremely efficient at its job and it can end a violent encounter with speed, stealth and accuracy.

One of the features that make the karambit such an effective weapon is the fact that the karambit is not a tool for stabbing and slicing, but rather ripping and tearing. Not only will the karambit sever veins, arteries, muscle and bone, but it will leave behind painful and jagged wounds because of the hooking and raking motion that the karambit makes as it 'bites' into the attacker.

Because of the curved design of the blade as it punctures the target the karambit will dig in and maintain a constant depth throughout the entire cut.

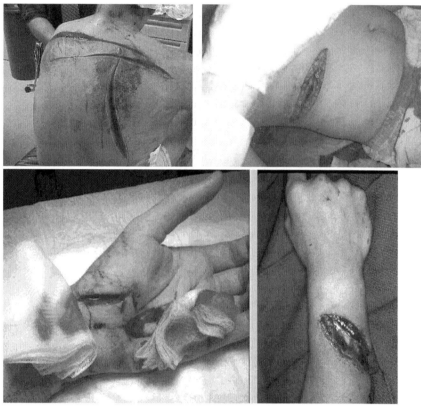

Note that the blade is a very dangerous weapon and not to be taken lightly

This will have a tremendous effect on your attacker considering that the more severe or traumatic the injury, the greater the fear, shock or pain that is experienced.

This can be an important factor during an attack, for with the advent of a huge adrenaline dump during an altercation the pain tolerance increases.

Often in a stress or combative situation, the people involved don't even realize that they have been injured until much later after the event has passed. You see this happen in car accidents and mishaps in the home, police chases, military operations or even while playing sports.

*****

Now if you are carrying a fixed blade (a knife made of one piece of metal) all that you need to do is practice deployment of the blade in a smooth fashion without injuring yourself or getting it hung-up on your clothing.

If on the other hand, you want to carry a folder (a knife that opens and closes, e.g. pocket knife) then there are many variations and types of opening devices available for the karambit. Actually, these mechanisms are available on all folder type knives.

Thumb Stud - One of the first methods for one handed opening was the thumb stud. The stud looks like the head of a socket cap screw and it is actuated by pushing up with your thumb in order to open the blade with one hand.

A problem with this type of opening device is that it only works for the right hand unless a stud is added to both sides.

Another issue is that the stud is fairly small and actually digs into the thumb when opening the blade which can be quite uncomfortable and the stud will tend to snag on your pocket and clothing when trying to deploy the blade.

Thumb stud

Thumb Plate - The thumb plate operates in the same manner as the thumb stud, but the plate sits on top of the back edge of the blade making for a cleaner design.

Besides being more aesthetically pleasing and having a better feel to it, the thumb plate is easier to access with the thumb and allows for smoother opening. Since it lays across the top of the back edge of the blade, it also allows for use with the left or right hand.

Thumb plate

Thumb Hole - The thumb hole is just that, a hole cut through the blade itself. The can be round, half moon, oblong or any similar shape. The idea is to press your thumb against the hole so that the pad of the thumb is pushed into the hole and then by flicking the thumb upward you open the blade.

This is one of the easier methods and can also be used in the reverse by holding the blade between the thumb and forefinger and 'flicking' the knife causing the handle to drop down and open the karambit.

Thumb hole

Holding the thumb hole by the blade to open

Wave - A wave opener has a proprietary notched design (like the crest of a wave) protruding from the back edge of the blade. When you pull the karambit out of your pocket by holding on to the retention ring the "wave" catches on the corner of your pocket and snaps the blade open automatically. This is a great piece of engineering and design.

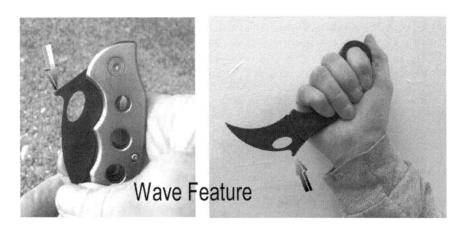

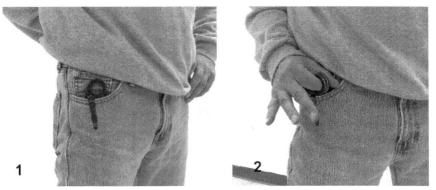

To use the wave feature you simply grab the karambit by the ring and pull up, applying a slight forward pressure (#2)

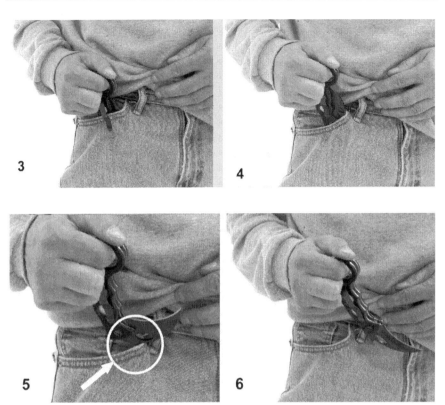

As the wave feature catches on the corner of your pocket it will pull the blade open as you continue to withdraw the knife.

Flipper - The flipper also has a notched protrusion, but this one juts out of the spine or top part of the handle. To release the blade you pull back on the "flipper" with your thumb or index finger, from here the ball bearing or spring assist will help to snap the blade into position.

Flipper

We should also look at the locking devices on the pocket knife karambits. We will take a look at four main types of locks for the blade.

Liner Lock - The first one that we will look at is the Liner lock. The liner lock is probably the most used and well known locking device for folding knives and was created in the 80's.

The liner lock works when one section of the liner inside of the frame is angled toward the middle of the frame opening or the center of the knife handle.

When the blade is deployed the liner slides over and under the bottom of the blade, holding it in place. To disengage the lock, the liner is manually pushed to the side away from the blade bottom allowing the blade to fold back into the handle.

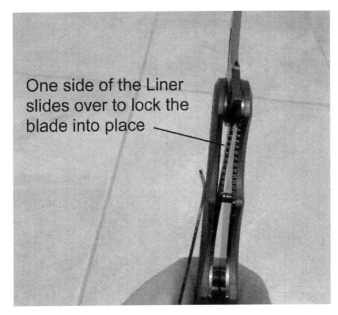

One side of the Liner slides over to lock the blade into place

The liner lock helped to advance the development of the tactical blade and the ability for one handed use of the pocket knife.

Frame Lock - Another similar locking device is the Frame lock.

The way that the frame and liner lock are different is that the frame which is also the handle actually make up the lock. As the karambit is opened one side of the frame (which is bent or angled inwards) will snap into place under the bottom edge of the blade locking it into place.

Since this lock is made from the handle or frame itself, it is a thicker piece of steel and thereby stronger than a liner lock.

Secrets of the Karambit

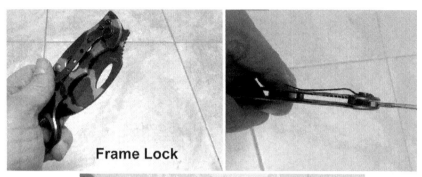

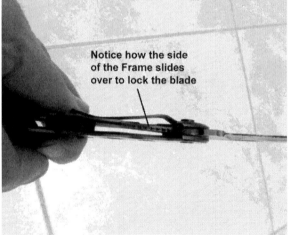

There are a few other locking types of lock that are proprietary such as the Axis Lock and the Tri-Ad Lock that have gotten very good reviews for their strength during fail tests.

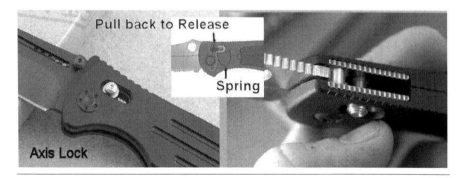

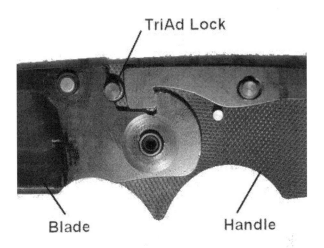

Now of course don't forget that there are also many utilitarian uses for the karambit such as those who use it for work, EMT's, camping, hiking or other activities.

The karambit was originally designed as a multi-purpose utility knife. While the karambits features effortlessly lend themselves to combative and tactical use it was not specifically designed for fighting.

For centuries, both the Filipino and Indonesian karambits have been used as an everyday carry (EDC) utility blade that could also double as a weapon when the need arose. Even today, many emergency personnel carry a karambit to use on the job as they also come equipped with a seatbelt cutter and glass breaker.

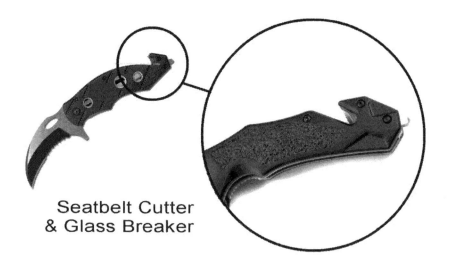

Seatbelt Cutter & Glass Breaker

If you are in a field such as Search and Rescue, EMT or something similar you may also want to look at a straight edge vs. a serrated edge. While a straight edge will give you a cleaner cut a serrated edge will be helpful if you are going to need to saw through something, this is why many blades have a clean, straight edge on the front edge of the blade and the back edge of the blade is serrated.

After you decide what style of karambit, which opening and locking mechanism you want I highly recommend that you also purchase a 'trainer' for practicing before you start drawing and striking with a live blade.

Training blades are manufactured in the fixed style or as a folder and can be made of wood, plastic or aluminum and can be found at many knife and martial arts stores, online or even at local flea markets.

Chapter 5

Grips

The basic grip of the karambit is to hold it with the blade pointing downward extending from the bottom of the fist, usually curving forwards, however occasionally it is held with the blade facing backwards and the index finger placed through the retention ring.

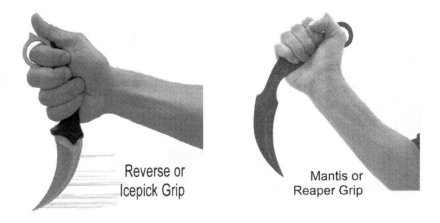

Reverse or Icepick Grip

Mantis or Reaper Grip

This is typically called the reverse grip, underhand grip or 'ice pick' grip. While it is primarily applied in a ripping, slashing or hooking motion, the karambit can also be used to punch the enemy and depending on the curvature, driving the blade into him in a linear and or hooking fashion.

You can also reverse the blade direction to what some call a 'Mantis' or 'Grim Reaper' grip, but most find it very awkward and you rarely see anyone use this unless you have a blade that is specifically designed for this type of grip.

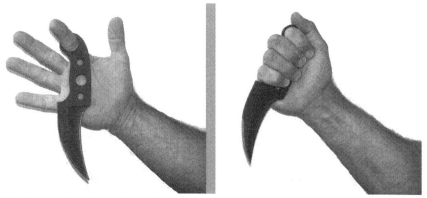

This karambit is made to be held in the reaper grip

The retention ring can also be used as a striking implement by hitting with a reverse hammer fist strike and using it in the same manner as a palm stick. The safety ring also makes the karambit difficult to disarm and allows the knife to be manipulated in the hand without losing one's grip.

Now it is not mandatory to place the index finger in the safety ring, you can just grab it by the handle if you prefer or if that is how it happened to deploy into your hand.

I have known some instructors who teach students not to use the retention ring, noting that your finger can become trapped in the ring and broken, but if your opponent is that good then you shouldn't be fighting with him in the first place.

As stated earlier the karambit blade design is based on the claws of the tiger and the blade forms a quarter moon shape. This shape allows for greater torque and cutting power in the reverse or underhand grip.

Using the blade in this fashion can generate tremendous power and allow the user to cut through flesh, muscle and even bone.

The karambit can also be held in the forward, overhand or 'hammer' grip with the blade on top looking like a big question mark. When held in this fashion the user greatly increases the speed of his strikes because it is used in more of a raking or slicing fashion, although held in this position it doesn't have the same penetration factor as the reverse grip.

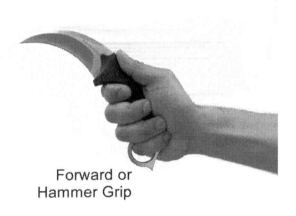

Forward or Hammer Grip

Utilizing the blade in the forward grip not only allows for greater speed, but greater versatility, hooking and reaching abilities with the knife. The forward grip, while not the preferred grip for most (mainly because of what they see in movies) is actually easier to manipulate and feels more natural because of the way that the hand and wrist move.

If you are using a fixed blade you may have the additional bonus of having a double edge, with an edge on both sides of the blade you are cutting and slicing with every movement and every block.

When used in this fashion (hammer or forward grip) the pinky finger is placed in the retention/safety ring. You can either close the thumb over the fingers as in making a fist or place the thumb on the thumb rise of the knife blade.

The third way of using the karambit is the extended grip, this is where you flip the blade out and away from you while retaining your grip on the retention ring between the index finger and thumb thereby allowing you additional reach for your strike. This is used as a slashing or raking movement, but has little penetration value as it is very difficult to apply any pressure when holding the karambit in this fashion. Typically, these strikes are aimed at the neck, groin or wrist.

Extended Grip

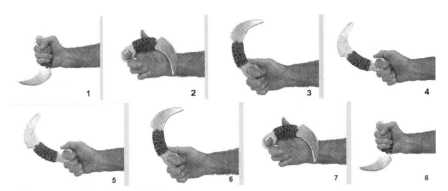

Flipping to the extended grip

Every karambit grip offers distinct advantages and disadvantages, by exploring the various options and familiarizing yourself with them you can decide which grip you prefer.

Much of this is dependent upon the way in which you carry and deploy the blade, but again this can be better determined after working with the knife and finding out what works best for you.

In addition to practicing the various grips, you also want to spend time working on the deployment and being able to transition the karambit in your hand to the preferred grip. In a high stress situation you will not have the luxury of taking the time to make sure that everything is just as you like it.

Switching hands or grips with the karambit is not as difficult as people think and it is actually more secure because you can keep a firm grip due to the retention ring until the blade is moved to the other hand or the grip changeover is made.

Secrets of the Karambit

Grip Change #1   #2   #3

To switch from a reverse grip to a forward grip you turn the right hand counter-clockwise (#2), placing the blade into your left palm. Switch the karambit to the left hand and twist your hand clockwise so that the thumb is facing downward.

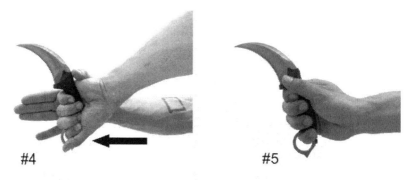

#4   #5

Come over the top with your right thumb while pushing the right hand forward and release the karambit into your right hand (#4). You are now in the forward grip.

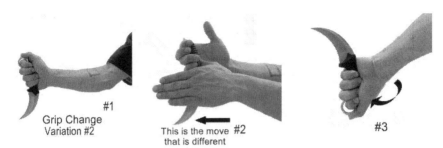

#1 Grip Change Variation #2
#2 This is the move that is different
#3

The 2nd way to change grips starts the same way, but instead of turning the hand over and placing the blade into your palm you keep your hand vertical and slide your left thumb between the handle and the palm of your hand (#2), sliding your left hand forward while grabbing the karambit. You then turn the left hand over (the same way as before) #3

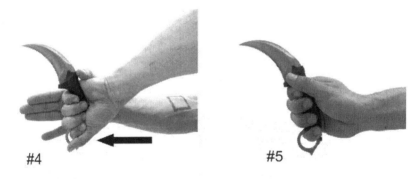

#4 #5

and proceed with the grip change just as in the first variation.

*****

Spinning the karambit can be fun and flashy, but you also need to take care, especially when working with a live blade.

If you are not familiar with the workings of the karambit or get distracted while twirling it is very easy to embed the point of the blade into your forearm.

I have seen many students and classmates do this over the years and even I have managed to flip the blade into my own forearm when I first began learning to manipulate the karambit.

You see this happen all the time at Knife Shows and Martial arts events, someone will walk over the sales table, grab a karambit, slip their finger in the ring, spin it and follow up with a quick yelp as the tip of the blade finds its mark in their arm.

Learning to spin the karambit should always be practiced with a training knife (you can learn from my mistake) until the user has sufficiently refined their skills and developed their hand coordination enough to consistently rotate the karambit trainer with precision and control.

You should be able to spin the blade in any direction (forward, backward, horizontal and vertical) without causing injury to yourself. When performing this maneuver you are learning to determine the weight and balance of the karambit, use the proper momentum and hand coordination to get the blade to perform as you wish.

Spinning the karambit is not for show, but to allow the blade to be used in combat to gain access to targets that would otherwise be out of reach such as cutting to the far side of the adversary's neck or the back of the leg.

If you don't get the proper momentum while rotating it, the blade will not be able to make a full revolution. As the blade rotation starts to diminish the blade will waver to one side or the other and it can cause it to bury itself in your arm, but the main issue is the angle of the karambit.

If the retention ring is situated on the middle joint (medial phalange) of the index finger, when you attempt to 'flip' the karambit, because of the angle that the blade is traveling it is much easier for the blade to embed itself into your arm or at the very least scrape down the entire front portion of your forearm.

Wrong Way to Flip
the Blade

Notice that when it is held on the middle phalange of the finger the angle makes it more susceptible to embedding itself into your arm.

The retention ring needs to be on the main portion of the finger between the base of the knuckle and the first joint (proximal phalange).

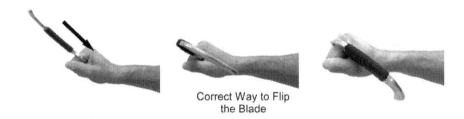

Correct Way to Flip
the Blade

Rather than trying to spin your karambit when you get it, try instead to begin familiarizing yourself with the various karambit grips and their uses.

Chapter 6

Deployment

As important as it is to choose the correct type of karambit it is equally important to know how to properly deploy the knife.

Karambit attacks are swift, sharp, deadly slashing attacks like a cheetah bringing down its prey on the Serengeti, by the time that you see it coming....it's too late. People who are skilled with this knife can draw it quickly and smoothly, deploying the blade, slicing and returning it to its sheath before you can bring your arm up into a defensive position.

The Karambit can be transported in a number of ways and positions on your person. What is best for you is an individual matter and depends on your needs and intended usage.

The karambit can be carried in your pocket (concealed or not concealed), in a sheath on your waist (inside or outside), in your shoe or boot, strapped to the thigh or with a lanyard around the neck.

It can be positioned on the right side (If you are right handed) to instantly load a reverse grip or on the left for a cross-draw which will put the karambit in a forward grip.

The next decision that you want to make is how to deploy the knife, do you want the handle up (ice pick grip) or handle down (hammer grip). Speed of deployment and ease of use is your primary goal, once you decide on and pick a style, stick with it.

After you settle on where to carry your karambit you need to remember to always carry the tool in the same place so that when you need it you are not struggling to remember which pocket, waistband or shoe you placed the blade in today.

In an emergency, you need to be able to go to it automatically, without thinking about it. It needs to become an automatic reflexive motion.

One way to help alleviate some of the deployment issues with the folder is to make sure that your karambit has a clip on the handle. This way you can clip it to your pocket, waist or wherever you decide to keep it, so that you know exactly where it is instead of having to fumble in your pocket or bag searching for it.

Although this will allow you to keep the karambit in a consistent location it is not foolproof. For example, if you carry your knife in your pocket or waistband and are seated in a chair at a restaurant or sitting in your car, it is now more difficult to access your karambit.

In a restaurant you would need to push away from the table and get to a standing position. While seated in your car, you will need to scoot your lower body forward and raise your hips or recline the seat in order to draw the weapon. This may not be easy to do in a stressful situation such as an accident or assault.

This is not to say that this is an unacceptable place to carry the karambit but just something to be aware of as no location is 100% perfect.

When you make up your mind which type that you prefer, you will also need to spend time practicing deployment of your karambit. Not only do you want a smooth draw, but you also want to make sure that you have a secure grip, ready for immediate use.

You practice for speed, for ease of deployment and for safety. With a fixed blade you will need to make sure that you don't snag your shirt, pants pocket or even slice your fingers or arm as you withdraw the blade.

A folder has these same concerns, plus you need to concentrate on becoming proficient with getting the karambit open. This can be a little tricky, but it is much easier today than in years past due to innovations in blade design.

And while a fixed-blade knife has no moving parts and is less likely to break, a folder, while being more convenient and easy to carry may not stand up to the stronger forces placed upon it during stress and could potentially fail.

*****

One last thing about practicing with your karambit, practicing doesn't mean doing the move 5 or 6 times and then you are an expert.

In order to get a movement into your muscle memory it needs to be practiced hundreds of times (ideally 1,000 - 2,000 to encode it into the muscle memory) so that it becomes second nature and you don't need to think about it but only to react. To become an expert you need to practice it 10,000 times.

Seems like a lot? That's ok, you don't have to practice to this extent, there will always be those who excel and those who are mediocre in every field, decide which one you want to be.

NOTES

Chapter 7

Types of Karambits

The modern western incarnation of the karambits design has changed very little from the original conception and while it can and is still used as a utility tool, the modern karambit is manufactured in a multitude of styles and design options as well as having a host of materials to choose from.

The two major designations that modern karambits are divided into are the fixed blade and the folder or pocket knife.

Within these two classifications you can also find variations such as boot knives, paracord or lanyard neck knives and others.

The fixed blade is obviously stronger and is able to take much more abuse than a folder since it is made of one piece of steel plus there is the added bonus of being able to put an edge on both sides of the blade. This isn't always the case of course, but it is more common to see a double edge with the fixed blade especially those found in Southeast Asia.

Deciding what type of karambit (fixed or folder) and where to carry it will be determined by what you want to use it for in your day to day activities.

A fixed blade can be drawn more smoothly and quickly than a folder because you don't have to open the blade first, you simply draw and slash. A folder takes a second or two longer, but is more convenient to carry.

If you decide that you want to carry a knife on your person, make sure that it is not too large as to make it cumbersome to transport, yet large enough so that it is sufficient for the job at hand.

If it isn't easy, useful or convenient to carry then in time you will stop bringing it with you and knowing Murphy's Law, when you leave it at home, you will come across a situation where it is needed.

One type of karambit that is small, out of the way and conceals well is the Neck Knife. The neck knife is hung around the neck and worn under the shirt and held in place by a paracord, beaded chain or lanyard of some type.

The neck knife is easy to carry and access by just reaching up under your shirt and pulling the blade free from its sheath and it doesn't get caught or bound up on clothing if you are in a seated position the way one in your pocket or attached to your waist would.

There are disadvantages of course, such as, the knife moves around when walking or running and additionally, if you are in a prone position it can slide to one side or the other making it difficult to find in an emergency.

If you choose to wear a neck knife, but there is a possibility that you may find yourself in hazardous situations such as what people in the military or working around machinery may encounter, you may want to consider a breakaway chain so you don't end up being choked with your own service implement.

NOTES

Part 2 - Karambit Basics

To view video clips of some of the following drills and techniques go to:

https://goo.gl/YEuuQR

Chapter 8

Being Responsible

If you are carrying a karambit for use as a utility tool on your job or for recreation (EMT, construction, military, hunter, backpacker, etc...) that is one thing, but if you carry for self-defense then you must be aware that restraint is necessary.

Just as with a gun, you cannot pull your weapon anytime someone annoys you, verbally assaults you or display it solely for intimidation purposes. If you must deploy your weapon in a defense situation be prepared to utilize it and be certain that you or your loved ones lives are in danger of imminent attack.

Deploying a weapon could diffuse a situation, but it could just as easily cause it to escalate and if you are the first one to display a weapon during an altercation, then you could be construed as the aggressor even if he started the confrontation.

If the incident is just about your ego, then let it go, if it is over your wallet or phone, give it to them, but if your life or the lives of others are in danger then the response must be swift and violent. Don't warn them, don't display the karambit and wave it around as this only gives him time to prepare or pull his own weapon and you don't want that to happen.

In a knife fight everyone gets cut. If someone tells you that they can teach you techniques to disarm a knife without any harm to you then they are either lying to you or painfully naive.

If a knife is in play..... you will get cut, the only question is how badly and who comes out on top. If you must brandish a weapon that means that conversation has failed and at this point you must eliminate the threat quickly and completely.

Occasionally you will hear someone say that a weapon is not needed to defend yourself or that real men don't carry weapons, I beg to differ, as we are not talking about school yard fights here, we are talking about life and death.

I've even heard other instructors talk about not teaching usage of the blade against an unarmed opponent. All that I can say is that these people are being myopic and short-sighted. When your life is on the line you do whatever it takes to survive, they attacked you remember?

Using this brand of logic, are you saying that if a woman is being accosted by a group of men, she shouldn't use her karambit to defend herself and escape with her life and virtue intact? If a wife is being beaten by her abusive husband that she can't defend herself because he isn't armed?

If you chance upon a group of men beating and raping a woman, are these individuals saying that you shouldn't pull your weapon (whether a gun or knife) to help her because they are unarmed? You can try talking to them if you choose, but more than likely you will be their next victim. This type of thinking makes no sense to me. And here we are only talking about civilians, we haven't even begun to rationalize the justifications of a soldier during a military encounter.

However I digress, as that really isn't what teaching a student techniques against an unarmed person is about.

The people who espouse opinions like this misunderstand the basics of teaching. No one is saying to attack an unarmed opponent with a weapon, what you are teaching the student are the basics. You are simply showing the trainee the fundamental techniques to use so that they are able to engage an attacker.

First you teach them the basic techniques against an unarmed opponent so that they can get the fundamentals down. When the student gets better and more comfortable with the technique or drill you can slowly introduce the weapon.

It is much easier to learn the basic maneuvers against a training partner when you don't have to worry about dealing with his knife or gun. Learn to walk before you run.

*****

Now, another quick issue that I'd like to bring up is firearms or specifically a conceal carry permit. Many people will tell you that they would rather just carry a gun (having a conceal carry license) instead of messing with a knife or other weapon and while they may have a point you must also remember that there are 'gunfree zones' where this is not possible.

There is also the matter of the "21 foot Rule" also known as the Tueller Drill. The Tueller Drill was devised by Sergeant Dennis Tueller of the Salt Lake City, Utah police department way back in 1983.

The drill was a self-defense training exercise to determine what was the minimum distance that a police officer could safely allow between himself and an attacker, before it was too late to be able to brandish his own weapon. After testing the drill at different distances it was determined that 21 feet is the MINIMUM distance that can safely be allowed.

How can that be?

The drill works like this: The 2 trainees face each other at a distance of 20 feet apart while the person with the gun has it holstered (remember he's the good guy) and the knife is already in the bad guys hand.

At a predetermined signal the attacker runs full speed at the potential victim. The shooter must draw his weapon and shoot the attacker without backing up (if he backs up, he is adding distance and it is no longer 20 feet).

20 ft covered in 1.5 seconds

It was found that the attacker could travel the distance of 20 feet in 1.5 seconds! At 20 feet the shooter was able to fire the weapon and hit the attacker just as he reached and stabbed the shooter and at any distance closer than this the man with the knife was ALWAYS able to stab the shooter before he could be shot. That's how the determination of 21 feet was established as the minimum amount of distance for safety.

Now I tell this story not to say that guns are ineffective, but to demonstrate how dangerous and effective a knife can be. If you carry a knife, gun or any weapon...........know how to use it.

Once last point, just because you carry a weapon doesn't mean that you are indestructible. Attacks are quick, deadly and violent and you can't always get to your weapon in time to ward off your attacker which is where having adequate hand to hand skills come in handy, but that is another book.

NOTES

Chapter 9

Pre-empting an Attack and Situational Awareness

An attack can often happen suddenly, but in many cases there are usually 'tells' or indications that it is coming. Stay focused on what is going on around you, especially if you are in a 'heated discussion' with someone. Keep your hands up in a non-aggressive posture, hands open, palms slightly facing each other as if to say, "Look, I don't want any trouble."

You want to maintain distance and have your hands ready to defend or attack. The last thing that you want to do is to stand toe to toe with your arms at your side with someone intent on doing you harm.

If he decides to attack and you have your hands at your side while standing two inches apart and puffing out your chest, you will have no time to defend yourself, your eyes have to see the attack coming and relay it to the brain, then the brain tells the arms that an attack is on the way and to raise the arms up to counter the attack and.........well, it is just too late.

You simply don't have enough time to react because you let him get too close.

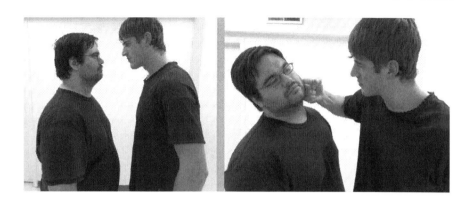

So keep the arms and hands up to maintain a proper distance and to give yourself a chance to cover if an attack comes, but be careful not to raise your arms with your hands balled into a fist, as it may cause the situation to escalate and it certainly will not look like you were trying to diffuse the situation to any potential witnesses that are around.

*****

Up until now you have been doing everything right, keeping your hands up, maintaining your composure, remain vigilant and staying calm, but it isn't enough. The aggressor is intent on assaulting you, pulls a knife from his front pocket and slashes.

Since your hands are already up, you only have to move your hand a few inches back to grab the back of your neck. This brings your arm over to cover and protect your face and throat (doing this also causes the shoulders to rise further protecting the neck).

Since roughly 80% of the population are right-handed, there is an excellent chance that the attack will be coming from the right (your left).

Ideally you should execute a right finger thrust to the eyes or throat at the same time (this is where your reflex training comes into play) yes, your arm will get cut, however that is better than your neck being sliced open.

Hopefully this will slow him up enough to wrap your left arm around his blade arm and head butt to the nose or drive a knee into the groin. If you can push or sweep him to the ground you want to pummel him until he is unconscious. Do not release his weapon arm until he is no longer a threat.

Your best hope in this situation if you cannot escape is to become the aggressor, go for the eyes, nose and throat until you can stop the threat. Don't grab for the knife because he will simply cut your hand, don't continually back away, sooner or later you will run out of room. If you can't run away you will have to close the gap (move closer) in order to stop him.

The knife isn't the problem, it's the person wielding it that you must stop.

In this type of scenario the universal concept to remember is evade, stop or stun, takedown and finish the attacker. It does no good to disarm them and not finish the job because they will simply get back up and finish it for you.

Never let up on your attacker until they are incapacitated.

Now this is only one quick example of many on how you could deal with this type of situation. When someone is trying to take your life you do whatever it takes to immobilize the threat.

Chapter 10

Karambit Striking Pattern

Note: to view video of some of the following drills and techniques go to **https://goo.gl/YEuuQR**

Now let's delve into the tactics for maneuvering the blade and actually start working on some basic movements.

Hand Positions - There are three basic hand positions for using the karambit, palm up, palm down and the vertical position. These positions will be the same regardless if you use the forward (hammer) grip or reverse (ice pick) grip.

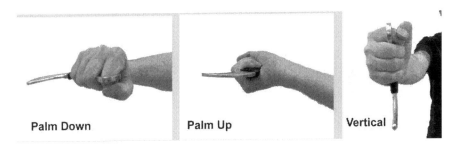

Palm Down   Palm Up   Vertical

Body Posture - There is no fancy position to jump into, no horse stance, no cat or crane stance, just maintain a natural posture like your typical boxing or MMA position. The only difference is that you want to keep your hand that is holding the knife to the rear. Don't place it out in front where the attacker can grab it.

Secrets of the Karambit

You've already chosen the style of karambit, and your preferred grip so we will start with the basic striking angles.

Now these angles will vary from system to system, but what we are showing you here are the strikes that we use and you will see that they cover every possible striking direction.

Angles of Attack - Angles #1 and #2 are diagonal down strikes, these rip downward from the shoulder to the waist, usually .....what most people don't understand or realize is that an angle #1 can be ANY diagonal down strike.

It can go from the shoulder to the waist, from the waist to the knee or knee to the ankle, the height doesn't matter, what matters is the direction of the strike.

Downward diagonal strike from right to left

Downward diagonal strike from left to right

Angles #3 and #4 are horizontal strikes, typically across the midsection but again, it can be any height. An angle #3 can slash across the eyes, the face, the neck, the midsection or....well, you get the point as long as it is horizontal it is an angle #3 or #4.

Horizontal slash

Reverse horizontal (note that the palm is facing up)

Angle #5 is a thrusting attack.

Angles #6 (from left to right) and #7 (from right to left) are diagonal up strikes from the knee to the waist or from the waist to the shoulder.

Diagonal up

Angles #8 and #9 are vertical strikes, angle #8 is a vertical down from the head to the groin and #9 is a vertical up, from the groin to the head.

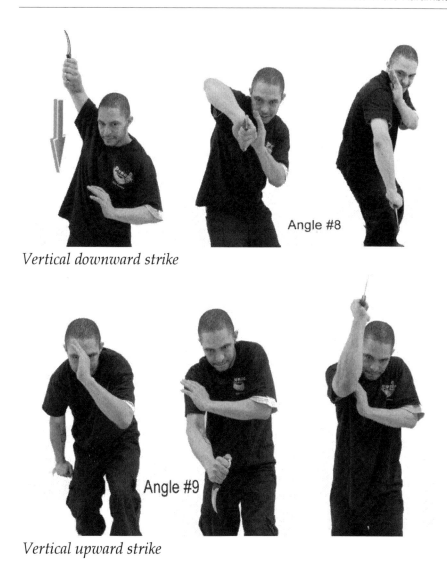

Vertical downward strike

Vertical upward strike

These nine attacking angles can be done with the forward (hammer) grip or the reverse (ice pick) grip, you can even practice them with the extended grip after a little practice.

Striking Areas - The following are basic striking targets, but remember, you are using a knife so any area that it touches will do damage.

#1) Carotid arteries and the trachea
#2) Femoral artery in the armpit
#3) Biceps

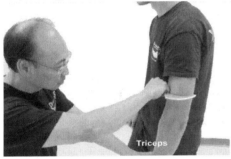
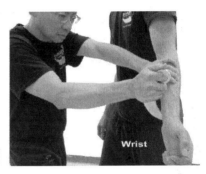

#4) Triceps
#5) Wrist

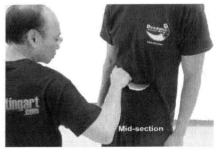

#6) Heart
#7) Abdomen

Low Line:

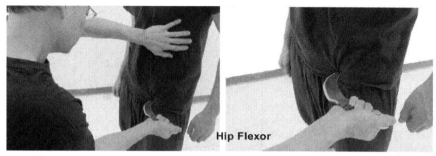

Hip flexor

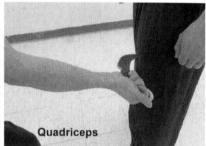

Quads and hamstring muscles

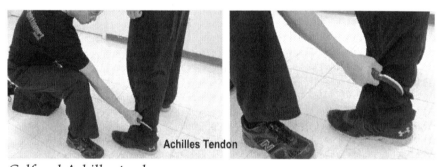

Calf and Achilles tendon

Neck Cuts:

 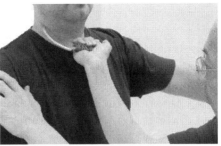

Unsupported cuts to the neck, these are simply quick slashes to either side of the neck.

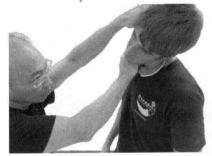 

Supported cut uses the free or 'live' hand to push on the head in order to apply more pressure.

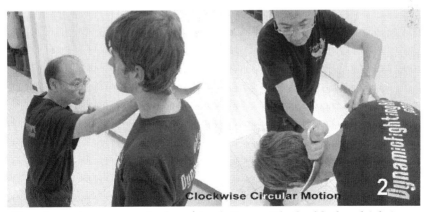

Circular cuts are a part of manipulation with the blade which is talked about later on. You actually use the karambit to push and control the head.

 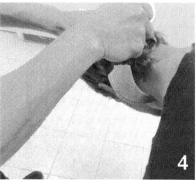

After forcing his head to move in a direction you step through to finish the cut.

Chapter 11

Blocking

Blocking with the karambit is extremely efficient because you don't actually 'block' the assailants incoming assault, but rather slash or cut the limb as the attack is being delivered.

If you have a karambit in your hand, you should not be 'blocking' in the traditional sense, but actually striking and slashing any part of his body that he tries to attack you with.

In fact, anytime that you have a bladed weapon in your hand it should be cutting. If you attack, defend, apply a joint lock, scoop or pass his arm, use destructions or entries, anytime your blade moves it should be cutting.

Now the type of 'blocking' shown is typically called 'Meeting the Force' because you are meeting his force or attack with an attack of your own. What we are showing here is Long Range blocking, there is also middle range and close range.

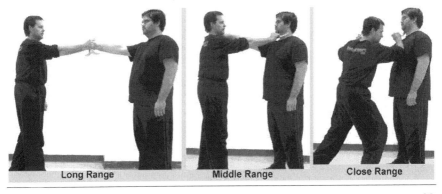
Long Range — Middle Range — Close Range

Long range is when your weapon is just able to reach the other person's arm. Middle range is when you can both strike or cut each other and close range is where you are able to grab your opponent.

The idea behind this type of 'blocking' is so that when he executes an angle #1 strike you will counter with an angle #1 and meet his attack, catching him on the inside wrist or hand and hopefully causing him to drop his weapon.

Blocking an Angle #1 Attack

The blades are moving in opposite directions, allowing you to catch his hand, wrist or forearm.

Blocking an Angle #2 Attack

Again, when he executes a #2 or backhand strike you will throw a backhand also thereby cutting his arm.

The idea is the same with the angle 3 and 4, the angle #3 is one of the more difficult to block because it can come in at any height and only the attacker knows where it will be thrown. Many times it is easier to aim for the bicep or even the face with this attack.

Blocking an Angle #5 Attack

You can move back or angle to your left.

Blocking an Angle #6 Attack

The angle 6 & 7 can also be tricky because you may also take a cut on the forearm if you are not careful.

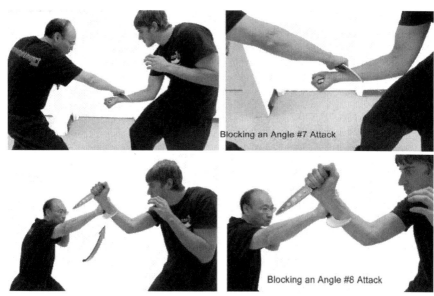

Be sure to move offline for the #8 (vertical downward) and not to stay underneath the attack.

Again, you want to move offline for the angle #9 attack

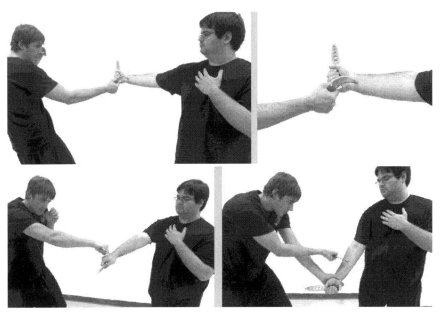

You should also practice the blocks using the forward or hammer grip position.

There is also Following the Force and Cross Body blocking.

Following the Force is a little problematic as you are 'blocking' in the same direction that the opponent is striking.

That is to say that if your opponent attacks with an angle #1 (his right to left downward diagonal strike), you would block by coming behind his strike and throwing an angle #2 (from your left to right downward diagonal).

This is more difficult because the attacker knows what strike he is going to attack with (1, 2, 3, etc...) , but you have to see it, recognize it and then try to intercept it from behind. These blocks are normally executed at long range and it is usually a little easier to catch anything coming from his left side (as in a backhand strike). Here are a few examples:

Following the force for an angle 1 and angle 2 attack.

Angle 3 & 4

Secrets of the Karambit

Angle 5 & 6

And finally angles 7, 8 & 9

Cross body blocking is used to better control a man with a blade by allowing you to keep the knife away from your body and vital areas.

When you block in this fashion, your body will twist at the waist and your arm blocks across your body from your right to your left with the palm up. This keeps the veins and arteries in the forearm away from the blade and allows you better control by providing constant pressure on his weapons hand thereby keeping the blade away from your body.

When executing the cross body block you want to maintain downward pressure to keep the blade away from your body. As the attacker slashes his strike will not stop but it will continue in an arcing motion to slice at your midsection. To avoid getting cut you keep downward pressure on his arm with your forearm, this will keep the blade away from your body.

Cross body block

Chapter 12

Entries

Entries allow you to safely move inside of your attacker's limbs to allow you to finish the encounter. Entries are usually defensive in nature, but that is not a hard and fast rule, entries can also be used to initiate the attack. An entry could simply be a block that allows you to block the assailants punch or strike and safely execute a counter-strike of your own, but to be efficient you don't want to block and then attack, you want to block and attack at the same time.

While there are many ways to do this one of the best and most used is something called muscle destructions or 'guntings' in silat and Filipino martial arts. Gunting translates as 'scissors' and it is a scissors like motion that you will make when executing these moves.

These are found in FMA, silat, kuntao and many other martial arts. You can block with one hand and simultaneously strike with the other or you can turn your block into a strike by moving your body offline and throwing out a single strike with enough force to disable the attacking limb.

Muscle destructions are based on the use of the knife and so fit perfectly in this instance. There are three basic destructions that we will look at:

The Outside Entry Destruction - The outside destruction is a parry of your opponent's strike and a simultaneous cut to the outside (triceps) of the attacker's arm. This can be done in an upward or downward slashing motion an upward vertical stabbing motion or even a horizontal stab depending on how you are holding the karambit.

As player 'A' attacks with a thrust, player 'B' parries and slashes upward, on the outside of the attackers arm.

From here he 'checks' to keep control of the arm while finishing with a cut to the throat.

Inside Entry Destruction - An inside destruction will also parry and strike at the same time, but this time you are going inside your opponent's defenses, meaning to say that you are moving inside between his arms.

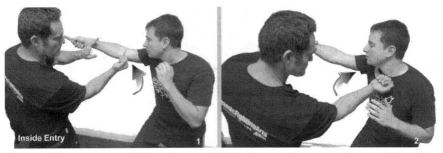

Player 'B' thrusts while player 'A' blocks and cuts to the inside of his arm. His left hand grabs to control the attackers weapon hand and finishes with a cut to the neck.

Split Entry Destruction - A split entry is when one of your hands is on the outside of his attack and the other hand is on the inside. For example, if the attacker throws a jab you would slip your head to the left and parry with your left hand, but your right hand is moving inside of his arm and cutting the bicep.

Player 'B' thrusts and player 'A' parries while simultaneously cutting to the inside of the bicep.

From here he continues a circular clockwise motion, bringing his hand on top of the arm. Now player 'A' can go straight to the neck or if he prefers he can 'fillet' the arm on the way up to the neck.

There are also other variations of these three, such as when attempting the inside destruction you attack the chest instead of the biceps with the blade. You could block with your left and stab or slash (depending on your grip) to the chest or midsection. When doing this technique without a weapon you would use your elbow in place of the blade.

variations

Another variation is the knuckle destruction (or slicer), this is a favorite of mine. As the punch comes in you would parry with your left hand and slash across the fingers of the fist with your karambit.

When using a straight blade you will slash all of the fingers when using this technique, but with the karambit the blade will hook and rip into the first finger on his fist that it catches, causing much more damage.

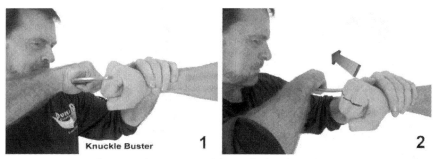

As you parry the punch you would guide his hand into your blade in order to slice across his fingers.

To do this technique without the karambit the right elbow would be used in place of the blade. When he strikes you guide his fist into your elbow hopefully shattering his fingers or knuckles.

NOTES

Chapter 13

Hand Grabs

When you deploy a weapon the first response of some people will be an attempt to grab it or the hand that is holding the weapon. Your initial reaction is to pull your arm away, but this won't work since you are trying to pull and slide your entire arm, wrist and hand through his fingers.

A better way is to simply pull or slap his forearm while lifting or pushing your weapons hand in the opposite direction. This way you are pushing your arm between his thumb and forefinger where there is much less resistance.

Don't pull straight back away from the attacker.

Secrets of the Karambit

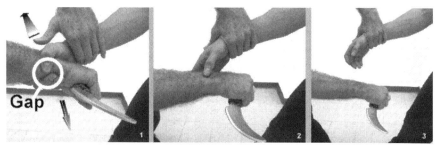

What you want to do is to lift his arm by slapping and pulling at the wrist while pushing the hand that is being grabbed through the gap between his finger and thumb in the opposite direction, pulling your arm free.

Quick Release #1 - Lift and push in the opposite direction. Remember to slap and pull his wrist fast and hard.

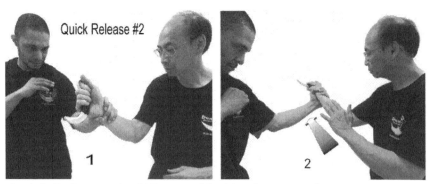

Quick Release #2 - When grabbed in the upward position you can rotate your arm outward.

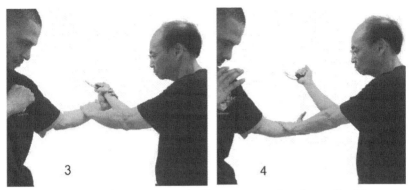

This will expose his wrist and allow you to firmly strike his wrist at a downward angle.

Quick Release #3 - *Again, push and pull. It helps to rotate the hand that is being grabbed as you push it towards him as you break free. You can also finish by driving the blade into your attacker as the karambit thrusts forward.*

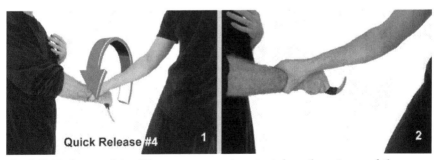

Quick Release #4 - *Here we are going to take advantage of the karambits unique design. As you are grabbed you simply spin the karambit upwards by releasing your grip starting with the pinky finger and flipping it up (this one takes a little practice).*

This brings the blade into position right above his wrist.

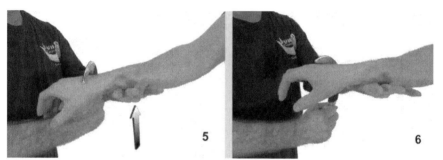

Now you slap his arm upward with your left hand while pulling down with your right hand, causing the karambit to slice his wrist.

The important thing is not to panic, by regular practice of these techniques you will automatically use a quick release when grabbed instead of trying to pull away from your opponent in the opposite direction.

Chapter 14

Footwork

Footwork is essential when using or facing a bladed weapon, good footwork separates the high-caliber fighter from the average fighter.

There are many types of footwork methods and many ways to train them. The three most common are: linear, angular and circular. All three types can be used for offensive and defensive movements and all three have their advantages and disadvantages in any given situation.

Linear footwork is simply moving in a straight line backward and forward or side to side, either by shuffling or stepping as in a walking fashion.

Moving backwards is ok to evade the initial attack, but sooner or later you will run out of space if you keep retreating. In addition by only moving in a straight line you are still in the 'line of fire' of the attack whether it is a gun, knife or fist. Moving to the side may be a better option depending on the situation as now you are 'offline' or out of the way of the attack.

If you move back to evade and then quickly move in to stop the aggressor, you will stand a better chance at surviving. In order to counter attack you must close the gap.

Remember: the knife, gun, pipe or hammer by itself cannot harm you, it is the person holding it who is the problem and must be stopped at all costs.

Angular or triangle footwork is a more advanced way of stepping and is extremely effective against an opponent with a weapon.

Angular stepping allows you to move offline and away from the trajectory of the weapon as well as provide an opportunity for closing the distance gap between you and the attacker.

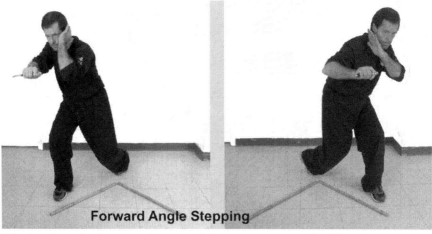
Forward Angle Stepping

Notice that the legs are bent and that you are not locking into a stance as you would in traditional martial arts. Your footwork must be fluid and flowing. This stepping allows you to move into your opponent.

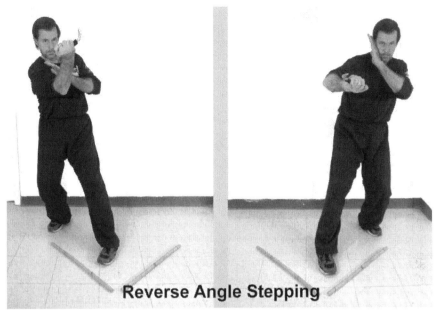

Reverse Angle Stepping

With this you move away from the attack while still using an attack of your own.

Notice how I step back to evade yet still am able to attack his limb.

This is just one example of many. As player 'B' attacks...

....player 'A' parries and blocks (you should always be cutting when you have a knife) while moving forward.

Here player 'A' steps out with his left foot to maintain a safe distance while cutting to the ribs.

Technique #2 *- player 'B' attacks with an angle #1, player 'A' steps back away from the strike while reaching for his karambit, and immediately steps forward with his left foot before 'B' can come back with the angle #4.*

To intercept the angle #4 strike 'A' moves even further in by stepping with his right foot as he blocks and cuts. Finally 'A' presses the attacker's weapon arm in order to finish the encounter with a cut to the neck. Notice here that we have used multiple angles in order to deal with this attack.

Circular stepping is another evasive stepping tactic that is difficult to employ, but if you can master the maneuver it can be very effective in countering your opponents attack by allowing you to move into his blind spot which, by the time he figures out where you have gone, it is too late.

Technique #3 - 'B' attacks with an angle #1 while 'A' uses a split entry as he steps to the outside.

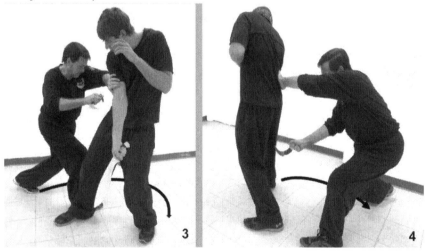

To continue his counter attack 'A' uses circular stepping to end up behind the opponent and finishes with a cut to the hamstring or groin.

Now one type of stepping is not necessarily better than another and most of the time they are used in conjunction with each other.

When attacking with the blade or defending against the blade you will find that footwork is an indispensable component to have in your arsenal. Remember, with a knife it only takes a 'touch' to do tremendous damage.

It is imperative that your body is in constant motion, moving from long to middle to close range and out again in order to avoid his attack or to mount a counterattack of your own, footwork is what will allow you to do this.

NOTES

Chapter 15

Solo Training

If you want to learn the karambit but don't have a partner and there are no schools around that teach it, there are ways to train on your own. Even if you do have a partner it is good to engage in additionally training on your own in order to perfect your skills.

There are always those who only do the minimum to get by in life and there are those who put forth extra effort in their training in an endeavor to increase their skills above and beyond their training partners or classmates.

One easy way to train at home is to get yourself a heavy bag or a standing bag to use as a target. If you want something l little more realistic you can purchase a 'Bob' dummy.

If lack of money is a problem, then you can grab an old tire and hang it from a tree limb or from the rafters in your garage or basement. If you live in an apartment or in the city you can simply go to the local park and practice maneuvering around a pole or tree. If you really want to learn something you can always find a way to do it. Those who make excuses really don't want to learn anyway.

Secrets of the Karambit

Working with the 'Bob' dummy

Drilling with old tires

Attaching a plastic pipe or water noodle to a pole. It doesn't have to be fancy or expensive to be effective.

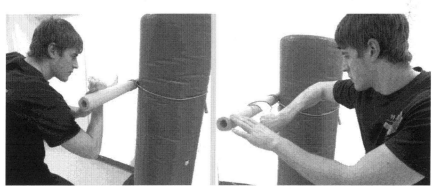

You can do the same thing with a hanging or standing bag.

Remember to always use a training karambit, if you don't have a karambit you can do most all of the same techniques with a straight blade by holding it in the ice pick position.

Individual training will help you to increase your strength, speed, flexibility, timing and reflexes. It will also help you to unwind from a stressful day and stimulate your mind which is helpful in other areas of life.

You will also gain new confidence by mastering this skill and you will know that if the need arises you will be able to defend yourself and your loved ones.

Chapter 16

Training Drills

Here we will show a few training drills that you can practice to help improve your skill with the karambit. When you are practicing your techniques make sure to train with intent, don't just walk through the motions.

Remember: the way that you train is the way that you will react on the street.

Striking Template - This template or pattern is an eight count drill to teach you vital striking points to attack.

This drill should be repeated many times starting off slow and then gradually increasing in speed until you are exerting your maximum effort.

Your partner can throw a punch, first right, then left for added realism, but you will find that after awhile this will slow you down when you begin increasing in speed because your partner won't be throwing the punches fast enough.

At this point you may just want to have him stand there with arms outstretched so that you can perform the drill as fast as you can with no delays.

Secrets of the Karambit

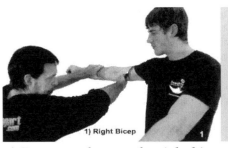 

1) Downward cut to the right bicep 2) Thrust to right brachial

3) Cut to left bicep 4) Thrust to left brachial

 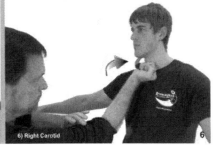

5) Slash to left carotid 6) Slash to right carotid

7) Thrust to heart 8) Slash to midsection

Pass & Scoop Drill - The idea of this drill is to teach you how to move your opponents limbs out of your way so that you can close the gap and enter into close range while still controlling his weapons hand in order to allow you to finish your counterattack.

Passing Drill - We are showing this with the karambit and straight blade. Player 'A' throws an angle #1 attack while player 'B' blocks using the back of his arm and slashes downward.

This puts him in a better position to pass the arm. A pass goes overhead in a clockwise rotation.

As player 'B' passes the arm overhead, he grabs it and slices downward.

Then player 'B' returns an angle #1, this allows player 'A' to block, cutting in a downward motion and then hooking the forearm for a pass overhead.

Here player 'A' passes, grabs to control and slices downward. From here the drill keeps repeating.

Scoop Drill - *For the scoop drill we are moving his arm in the opposite direction as before. Player 'A' attacks with an angle #1 and player 'B' blocks up instead of down(note that 'B' has changed grips). This allows him to immediately hook his blade on the opponent's arm.*

What we are looking for is expediency, you would not cut down, then cut up to scoop as that would be three moves and the arm may not still be in the same position. You want to simplify it, by cutting up and immediately hooking the arm and scooping to the low line in a counter-clockwise rotation.

Secrets of the Karambit

From here player 'B' grabs the arm (above the elbow) for control and slashes up. Then returns an angle #1 attack.

Player 'A' blocks, slashes upward, hooks the forearm.......

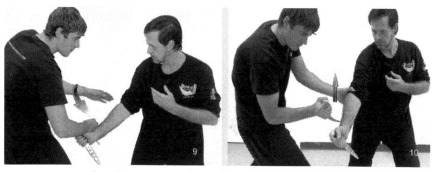

...scoops, grabs the arm and slashes upward. Repeat...

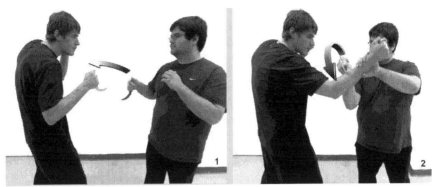

Scoop Drill variation #2 - *Player 'A' executes an angle #1 attack, player 'B' blocks and cuts up and hooks the arm with the karambit*

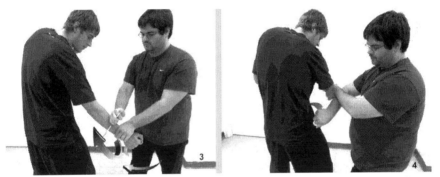

He then scoops, grabs with the left hand to control and slices to the ribs.

'B' then throws the angle #1 strike so that 'A' can return the favor, 'A' blocks and cuts up

Scoops the arm, grabs above the elbow to control and slices to the ribs.

More Advanced 2-man drills - These drills are a little more interactive as both men will give and take using different techniques during the drill.

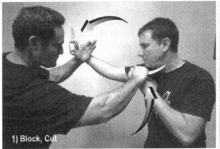 

Scoop Drill variation #3 - To begin the drill, player 'B' (on the right) throws an angle #1 attack. Player 'A' blocks and slashes at the same time (#1)

Player 'A' then scoops the arm and tries to cut player 'B' in the ribs (#3 & 4)

Not wanting to be cut, player 'B' steps back with his right foot, checks or blocks with his left and cuts player 'A's forearm then 'B' throws an angle #1 attack and the drill begins again.

Secrets of the Karambit

Scoop Drill variation #4 - *(notice the grip change on the karambit) The 2nd drill starts the same but as player 'A' scoops his partners arm, player 'B' quickly strikes at player 'A's face before he is able to cut player 'B's ribs.*

Seeing this, player 'A' must immediately deal with this oncoming attack by blocking and cutting and then replying with an angle #8. Player 'B' blocks the vertical attack with a roof block (block and cut straight across) and then the drill starts again.

Note: this drill can also go back and forth with each player alternating attacking and defending.

Three man scenarios (two attackers) - You can also create drills with multiple attackers to make it even more realistic. I would suggest using something like what is shown here before moving on to creating your own.

Keep them short and simple and start with a choreographed attack sequence before attempting random attacks. If you start right into random attacking there is a good chance that someone will get hurt because things can go downhill very quickly when multiple attackers are coming at you from all sides.

Multiple Attackers #1 - In this scenario player 'A' (in the middle) is attacked by player 'B' with a jab. 'A' parries and cuts using an outside entry

He then steps in and finishes with a cut to the neck.

All of this should take place in 2-3 seconds. Player 'C' now starts to move in as 'A' quickly turns to meet him

Player 'C' lunges with an angle #5 thrust, 'A' sidesteps and blocks

Scooping the arm and grabbing he finishes with a slice to the ribs.

Multiple Attackers #2 - 'B' again attacks with a jab as 'A' uses an outside or split entry (it's good to practice variations) and cuts the ribs ...

As he turns he sees that 'C' is already upon him so while still controlling 'B's arm he pulls 'B' in front of him to use as a shield and thrusts straight out to counter 'C's attack.

Multiple Attackers #3 - *This time the attackers are in a different configuration than before and both are attacking more from the front. As 'B' throws a left hook, player 'A' uses an inside entry, blocking with his left hand and cutting the biceps with the karambit...*

And quickly finishes with a neck cut, player 'C' steps in and throws a right hook which is also blocked on the inside...

Here 'A' scoops, spinning him around...

Which allows 'A' to move to the rear to finish the attacker. Notice how forcefully scooping the arm allowed him to manipulate the body into a more favorable position for a counter attack.

Be sure to wear safety glasses and use training karambits when practicing these type of drills.

NOTES

Chapter 17

Impact Strikes

This is something that most people never think about, using the karambit as an impact weapon. Why would you do this you ask? Perhaps as you grab for your pocket knife the aggressor attacks before you can get the karambit open.

Perhaps the altercation doesn't appear to be a dire enough situation to warrant the use of a blade or you just don't have it in you to cause someone permanent, serious injury or death.

You can choose to use the karambit as an impact weapon along with the retention ring if you should decide to minimize the damage done to your attacker.

Even with a fixed knife or the blade engaged on your folder you can still strike with the back edge of the karambit blade to strike (think that a piece of steel slapped upside your head won't hurt?) because once you've engaged the attacker you don't back-off or retreat. You want to make every strike count and you continue your counter-attack until the threat is stopped whether that is with the edge of the karambit or any other part of the weapon.

The reason that the back edge of the folder (having only one sharp edge on the inside of the blade) would be used as an impact weapon would be so that you don't interrupt the 'flow' of the blades motion.

Although the folding karambit can be used as an impact weapon when opened, you must be aware that the strength and safety of the blade is determined by the quality of the manufacturing process and materials used, therefore if you were to use it as an impact weapon (once the blade is deployed) one possible issue could be that the locking mechanism could fail causing the blade to close back on the user's fingers.

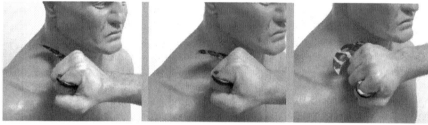

Folder failing

As long as you are striking you can impart damage or manipulate him into position for the finishing blow, but the karambit can be even more effective as an impact weapon before opening the blade.

*****

Impact strikes would predominantly be executed using a pocket knife style karambit rather than a fixed blade as you would use it gripped tightly in your hand like you would a palm stick, striking with both ends of the still folded karambit.

Using the karambit in this fashion can be devastating in the right hands because it is made of steel and will greatly enhance the power of your strikes.

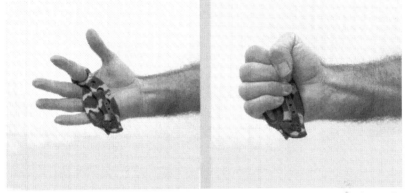

Using your folder as an impact weapon. Notice how nicely it fits into the hand and the retention ring keeps it secure while striking.

This is not to say that the fixed blade karambit can't be used. You can still use it as an impact weapon and strike with the back edge of the blade provided that it doesn't have a sharp edge and don't forget about using the retention ring.

A swiping blow to the temple, striking with the retention ring first would have tremendous knock-out potential as the power is concentrated at the end of the retention ring as it smashes into its target.

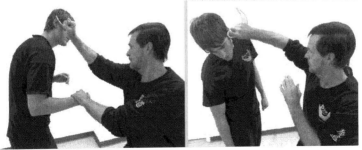

Impact strike using the back of the blade or the retention ring.

As stated earlier another reason to use impact strikes is to not impede the 'flow' of your striking attack. What that means is that your strikes with the karambit should not be a series of short stabbing, thrusting attacks or crude slashing, hacking strikes, but rather a series of flowing horizontal, diagonal, vertical and figure 8 type movements, this type of flow is typically referred to as the "dance of the karambit".

For example, if you slash from your right with a #1 or #3 your next move would be a #2 or #4, if you swing or slash the blade to the left then the arm must come back. You might as well hit something while bringing the arm back and if it is an impact hit instead of a cut, then that is fine as it will still do damage.

When using the karambit folder as an impact weapon you will strike with a hammer fist and also by using the retention ring in a similar fashion to throwing a ridge hand strike.

Your target areas are many: the temples, bridge of the nose, base of the skull, sternum, chest, arms, hands, legs, groin, anywhere that you can kick, punch or elbow is a viable target.

Using the karambit in this fashion maximizes the intensity of the impact of the strikes. It is like driving the end of a steel pipe or rod into them.

This type of striking is also used for pressure point strikes and pain compliance, which are both enhanced by the karambit simply due to the fact that it is made of steel rather than wood like many palm sticks.

Secrets of the Karambit

With slight modifications you can use the same entries and techniques, whether the knife is open or closed.

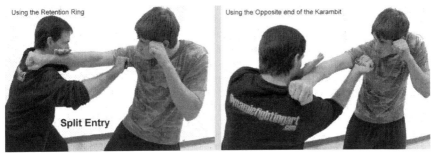

These are very devastating as you are driving a piece of steel into the muscle...

or the bone...

Just as there is a template for cutting there is also one for impact strikes.

Secrets of the Karambit

Impact Template - 'B' *punches with a jab and* 'A' *parries and strikes with the knuckle buster, the next strike is to the triceps.*

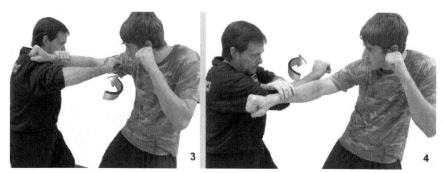

From here you strike the inside bicep (retention ring) and then the outside of the triceps (bottom of knife).

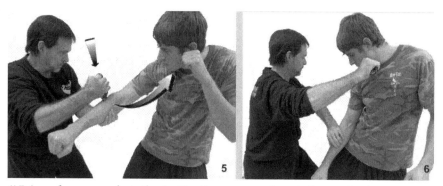

#5 is a downward strike to the forearm and a strike to the jaw.

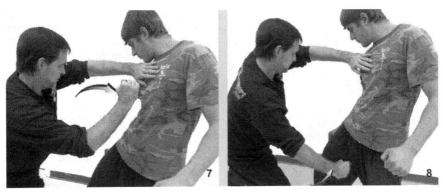

Finishing with a strike to the chest and a upward strike to the groin.

Notice how the ends of the karambit strike, you typically will bounce off of your targets and alternate the strikes from one side of the knife to the other side.

This drill is to teach you to keep the hand and weapon moving and flowing from one target to the next. The template teaches the different strikes and angles of flow and is not meant to imply that these are the only targets that are available for striking or that they need to be struck in this order.

Secrets of the Karambit

Impact #1 - *player 'A' jabs and player 'B' slips the punch while parrying and driving the retention ring into the triceps.*

'B' then moves in and drives the bottom of the folder into the biceps as the attacker is withdrawing his arm. Notice how he is 'cupping' the arm, this will help to maximize the power of the strike.

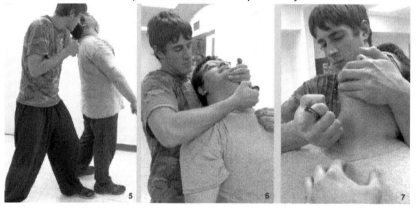

From here 'B' circles around to the back, grabbing the neck and driving the folded karambit into the trachea.

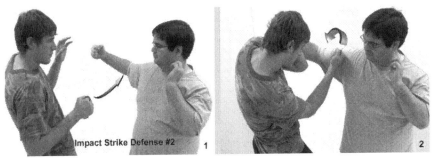

Impact #2 - *When 'B' throws a hook punch 'A' blocks and drives his fist or karambit into the biceps of the attacker...*

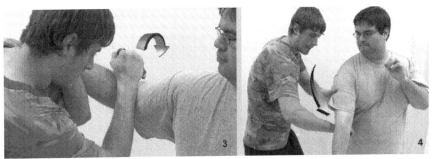

'A' scoops and maintains control with his left hand...

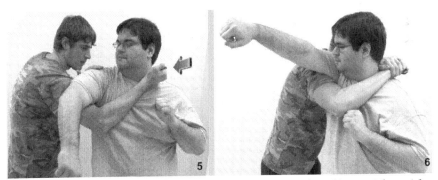

continuing to circle under the attacker's arm and ending with a side choke. You can drive the end of the karambit into the side of his neck if you want to...

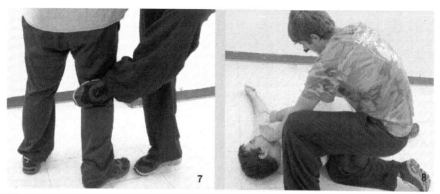

Next 'A', kicks the back of his attackers leg to bring him to the ground...

and finishes with multiple strikes to the body.

Secrets of the Karambit

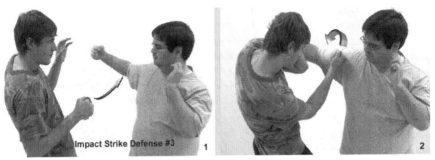

Impact #3 - *This starts off the same as before, when 'B' throws a hook punch 'A' blocks and drives his fist or karambit into the bicep of the attacker.*

'A' scoops and maintains control with his left hand,

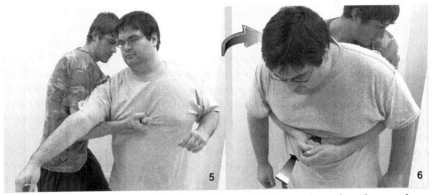

but this time 'A' drives his closed karambit into the solarplex and gives a sharp pull to drive the air from his lungs.

145

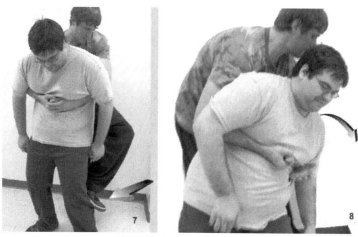

'A' again kicks and pulls his attacker to the ground...

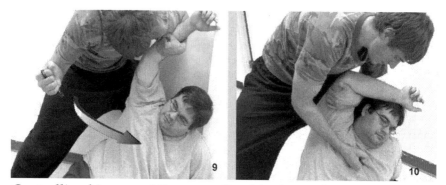

Controlling his arm while pummeling him into submission.

Secrets of the Karambit

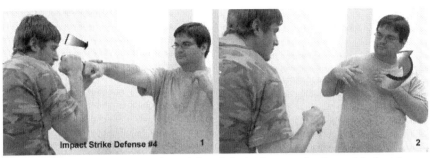

Impact #4 - *As 'B' attacks with a jab, 'A' uses the knuckle buster, as 'B' retracts his hand in pain*

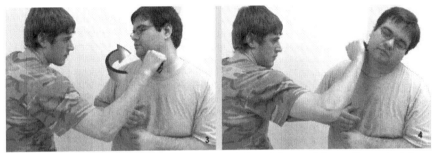

'A' follows the arm by moving in and finishing with strikes to either side of the jaw.

Impact #5 - As 'B' throws a hook or sucker punch, 'A' decides to try a different tactic by dropping to the low line and striking the groin.

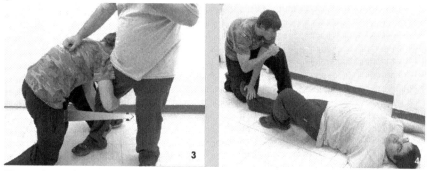

From here he applies a single leg takedown...

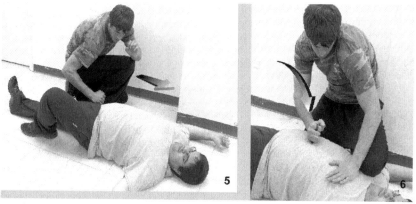

and moves up the body, striking as he goes.

Secrets of the Karambit

Impact #6 - *This is a variation of the single leg takedown. As player 'B' hooks, player 'A' drops to the ground while driving the karambit into the groin.*

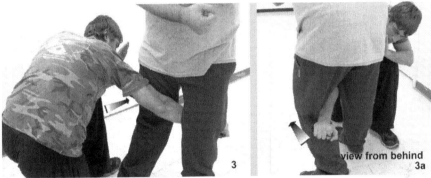

Next, he weaves his right arm between the opponent's legs, hooking the karambit behind the knee and driving forward with the right shoulder into the thigh while pulling with the karambit.

If player 'B' tries to kick, 'A' blocks and strikes the thigh with the karambit and passes the leg overhead...

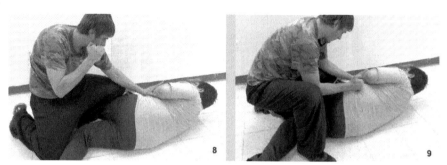

maintaining pressure to keep him off-balance 'A' finishes with multiple strikes.

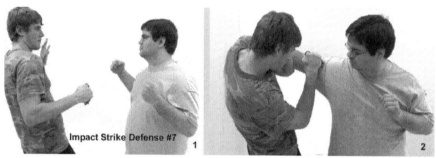

Impact #7 - *When 'B' hooks, 'A' does an inside entry striking the biceps*

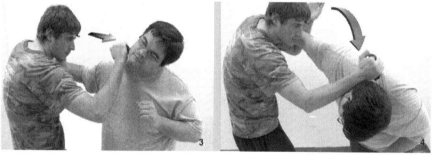

he then strikes to the side of the neck and executes a head spin. 'A' is lifting the arm while pushing down on the neck, forcing the opponent into the ground.

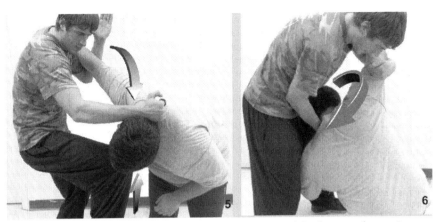

While forcing him down you drive a knee into his face and continue the spin...

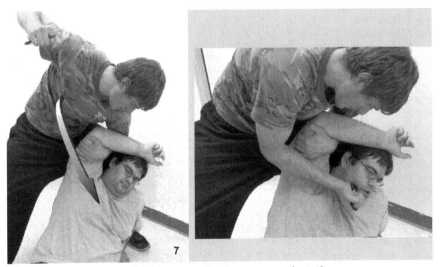

...once on the ground 'A' controls the arm and strikes.

When practicing the impact techniques it is best to use a short piece of wood like a dowel rod, a piece of wood covered with foam or just use a closed fist. I don't recommend striking your training partner with the steel karambit if you want to keep him around.

NOTES

Chapter 18

Body Manipulation

Body manipulation is based on the concept of choke and or control points on the body which are manipulated in order to disrupt the opponents balance. The karambit can be a dynamic tool used to make body manipulations more efficient and effective.

One currently well known method of these techniques come from the Filipino martial arts (FMA) and is referred to as Buno, Dumog or Combat Judo, of course, these same types of movements can be found in silat, kuntao and many other arts.

In order to better understand this concept we will take a closer look at dumog or buno. Dumog (as it is most commonly called) can be considered the grappling or wrestling component of FMA which utilizes grabbing, pushing, pulling, dragging, twisting, poking, weight shifting and joint locks to move your opponent off-balance to a more advantageous position for a counter strike. Most of the moves are executed while standing and it is not a ground art like Brazilian JuJitsu or Harimau Silat.

The techniques include, but are not limited to; hand and elbow strikes, knee and low kicks, throws, sweeps, joint locks, arm wrenches, arm drags, shoulder and hip bumps, choke holds, head cranks, pressure-point and come-along (controlling) techniques.

There are some roughly 20 control points that can be utilized to help you to manipulate, control and restrain your attacker. Now of course not all of these apply to the karambit, and we will be exploring them further in future books. They include:

Head - Control the head and you control the body.
Eyes - A quick poke will temporarily disable the attacker.
Nose - Besides just smashing the nose you can easily move the head by pulling on it (this comes in handy for making an access path for a choke).
Ear - You can pull or rip (and if they have piercings, ripping one out will surely get their attention).
Jaw - Many pressure points along the jaw line.
Neck - Many arteries and nerves to attack. You can also apply twisting, cranking and choking maneuvers
Throat - A quick strike will inhibit the ability to breath.
Shoulders - Pushing and pulling the shoulders enables you to reposition, twist and shift your opponent into position.
Bicep - This can be struck as in a muscle destruction or manipulated using a push/pull motion
Tricep - Same as bicep
Elbow - Control the elbow and you control the arm
Wrist - Good for twisting and joint locks
Fingers - Bend, twist or break, good for pain compliance
Solar Plexus - Strikes to the solar plexus or xiphoid process can cause immediate gasping for breath or lacerations to the diaphragm.

Groin - Groin strikes can immediately drop your attacker to his knees in excruciating pain, this strike will also work on women.

Hip Flexor - Striking this area allows you to move, bend, twist and takedown the attacker

Knee - The knee-joint supports the body, if you hit, strike or destroy the knee and the attacker is down.

Ankle/Achilles - Strike or cut here and the balance and support are gone.

Instep - A stomp with hard soled shoes will bring about instant results. The metatarsal bones in this region can be easily broken, making it impossible for them to walk or run

Toe - Stomping on the toes will cause extreme pain or even break them.

Using control points will help to 'open up' your attacker by moving an arm, leg or turning his body, giving you a more advantageous angle from which to counter attack.

For example; if the attacker throws a right hook you can 'scoop' the arm in a downward, half-moon or counter clockwise arc in order to turn his body and position yourself to his right, allowing you an opportunity for a counter strike without fear of him being able to strike back. By scooping his arm you move or twist his body, making it more difficult for him to throw another right or even a left-handed attack.

These types of control techniques will allow you to 'move' your attacker into objects in the environment such as a wall, pole or vehicle. You can also position them to be used as a human shield against multiple attackers or escort them from the area using controlling, pain compliance or come-along techniques.

Most of the areas attacked with the karambit will be joints: neck, shoulder, elbow, hips, knees and such, but muscles will work well also. If you want to get him to move and drive the tip of your blade into his thigh (quads) his leg will move faster than even he thought possible.

As you will see below the blade is also used in conjunction with the other arm in order to move or control him.

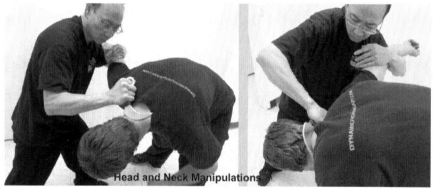

Head and neck manipulations

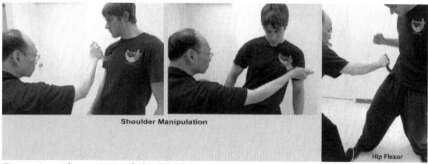

By using the point of the blade you can cause him to move where you want

Secrets of the Karambit

Arm drag manipulations

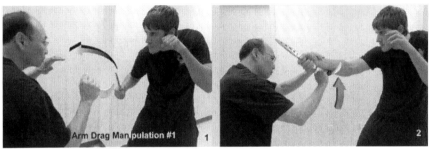

Manipulation #1 - Player 'B' throws a thrust or an angle #1, player 'A' uses a split entry to counter

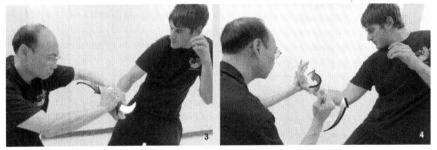

Maintaining the grip with the left hand player 'A' strips the knife from 'B's grip and executes a wrist lock (wrist manipulation).

You are employing the karambit to execute an arm drag, by placing it in the crook of his elbow and pulling sharply down, it will bring him into position for a neck cut.

By using manipulation of the wrist and elbow you are moving him into the position where you want him in order to finish the encounter. This allows YOU to control the fight, not him.

Secrets of the Karambit

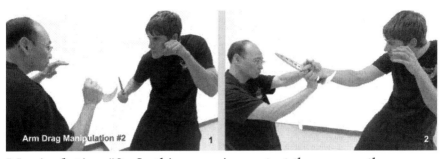

Manipulation #2 - *In this scenario we start the same as the previous encounter, but...*

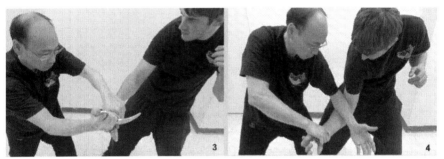

This time, after the disarm player 'A' uses his Left arm to apply the arm drag

Once again this maneuver will cause his head to jerk forward and pull him into your blade.

Manipulation #3 - *After player 'A' enters with a split entry, he digs the karambit into the crook of player 'B's elbow...*

Then he pushes straight back as hard as he can to remove the blade from play just long enough to slash across the mid-section

'B" then throws a left hook which 'A' blocks, cuts and scoops

From here 'A' grabs the arm and pulls to keep him off-balance (and it keeps the knife away) while slashing to the ribs.

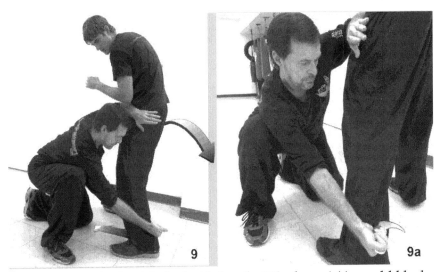

(If 'B' swings back with the knife (angle #3) player 'A' would block, scoop and disarm before the next move) If he doesn't attack then 'A' drops to one knee and hooks the ankle, he then puts the elbow into the hip flexor, or you can grab the leg with your left arm if you prefer and use your shoulder for the takedown.

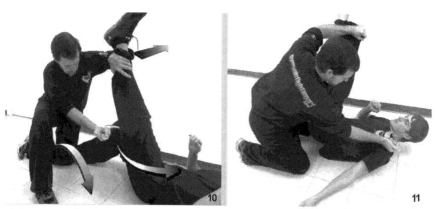

After completing the single leg takedown, he maintains pressure on the leg to keep him off-balance while finishing with a cut to the neck.

Now the scenario above, may or may not play out as shown. The point is to show the various ways to manipulate the body and keep a constant flow of counter-attacks while using the karambit.

If we take a closer look you will see that in fig. 3 the karambit is used to push the arm, thereby temporarily removing his knife from play. In fig. 6 the karambit is used to scoop and move the arm. And in fig. 9 the karambit is used to hook the ankle in order to assist in the takedown.

These are just a few ways to use the karambit to move and manipulate the body. If you look closely you will find many more throughout the book.

In order to win a street altercation you must control the situation and learning how to move your opponent will help you to do just that.

Chapter 19

Street-Defense

A violent encounter is not a game, it doesn't stop with a "tap out" or a winning point. There are no rules, no second chances and no referee to halt the attack. It will only end when either you or your attacker are dead or incapacitated.

It is always best to avoid violence, but that is not always possible, sometimes it finds you. The best defense is situational awareness, be aware of your surroundings, especially at night or in a questionable area of town.

This doesn't mean that you have to be paranoid, just use common sense. Don't walk alone at night in dark unlit areas, if you are in a restaurant or building, note where the exits are in case of an emergency, keep your car doors locked while driving, things like this. You've heard it before, but sadly, times just aren't as innocent as they used to be.

The biggest obstacle to street defense is ourselves. Most of us are decent, hard-working people who only want to get an education, find a nice job, get married, raise a family, enjoy life and then retire.

The problem is that not everyone thinks this way, not everyone shares the same ideas and values that most normal people have.

There are those who only want to take from you and from society as a whole, they feel entitled or owed something, are on drugs or simply don't care. They have no morals, no values, no compassion, no empathy, they are simply 'dead' inside. They live on the fringe of society and they see you as prey, simply another victim to use, take from and discard.

Many self-defense books, articles and experts will tell you to reason with them, but these are not reasonable people that we are dealing with, they are miscreants, the dregs of society.

They don't want to talk, they don't want a lecture, they want your money or your body to rape and or murder.

These people don't play or live by the same rules as the rest of us, so what would seem like a normal response to an assault may not work. If you can just hand over your wallet or purse then by all means do it, you can always make more money and credit cards can be replaced, but unfortunately, sometimes that isn't enough.

If it seems that you or your loved one's life is in danger then you cannot be indecisive, you must attack. If you delay, hesitate, or stop to think about it you will start to lose your nerve.

The counter attack must be swift and violent, and you must attack with twice as much aggression as the attacker has shown. In an evenly matched encounter the person who is more aggressive will usually win.

Remember, the people who are attacking you know nothing about fair play, they only know that they want to win at all costs.

This is why you usually see more than one criminal attacking a person. They don't care about being fair, they only want to make sure that the odds are in their favor and they want to take your money or your life at any cost.

Street scenario #1 - When 'A' is grabbed by the wrist to be dragged towards an awaiting car or van, she quickly reaches into her pocket to grab her karambit.

From here a quick slash to the arm should make the attacker let go long enough for her to make an escape. If he continues to pursue then she would follow up with further strikes.

If you are accosted on the street, then it is up to you to fight back and protect yourself.

You can't depend on passersby (how many stories have you read about someone being attacked and onlookers standing around doing nothing to help them) and you can't depend on the police, they can't be everywhere and by the time that they get to you it will be too late.

You have to do everything in your power to get away from an assailant, if you are dragged into a car or van the chances of getting out alive are not good.

Remember; No one has the right to touch, molest or assault you.

Here we are going to take a look at some common street attacks.

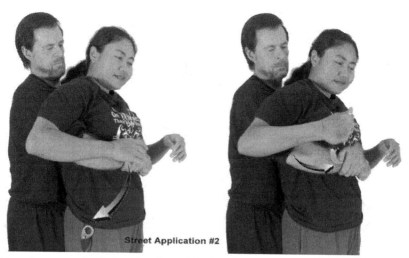

Street scenario #2 - Bearhug Under the arms
When grabbed from behind and dragged into an alley or vehicle, she reaches down and grabs her karambit,

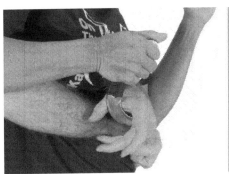

and either slashes the hand or inserts it between the hand and arm in order to dig it into the hand. This will work even if he lifts her off of the ground.

Street scenario #3 - *Bearhug Over the arms*
This one works basically the same because the lower part of the arm is still free to move. She simply reaches down and grabs her karambit to cut and slash the attacker.

Street scenario #4 - *If choked and shoved up against the wall the most important thing is not to panic. Pulling at his hands will not help, she must quickly grab her karambit and slice the wrist to release the grip.*

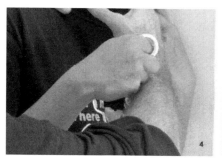 

Now finish with a throat cut if necessary to escape. (she seems to be enjoying that last move a bit too much)

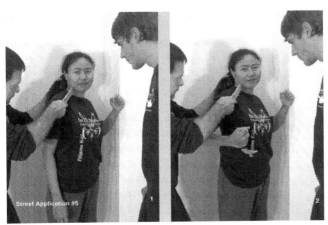

Street scenario #5 - *When accosted by two attackers again the key is to remain calm. Grab the karambit....*

...and push his hand to the side, from here she can stab the body or cut the wrist. Immediately stab the other attacker and run.

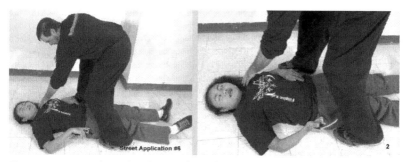

Street scenario #6 - *Being knocked to the ground is a dangerous situation to be in, but as the attacker is trying to control you he won't notice your hand discretely removing your karambit from it's place of concealment.*

She quickly slashes the nearest part of his leg that is available and continues slashing until she is able to escape.

Chapter 20

Zombie Apocalypse
(Empty Hand Training)

I mentioned earlier about how learning the basic techniques and drills against an unarmed attacker allows you to concentrate more on the techniques, your timing, your reflexes and spatial relationship to your training partner.

If you still find working with an unarmed opponent to be distasteful then you can think of it as fighting zombies during the apocalypse. But as I stated before, there is nothing distasteful about saving your life.

Zombie training #1 - Player 'B' jabs and it is intercepted with a split entry.

Here player 'A' cuts the bicep and then the ribs.

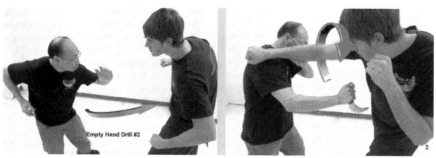

Zombie training #2 - Parry off of the jab with an immediate slash to the ribs.

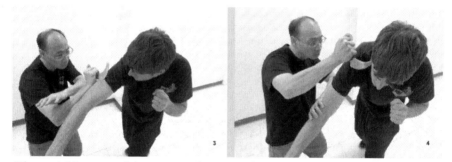

Player 'A' moves his arm to the outside to push and control with the karambit and the left hand, finish with a neck cut.

Zombie training #3 - *Using an inside entry to block the hook player 'A' cuts upward...*

Hooks the arm and scoops downward.

Here he grabs the arm (above the elbow for better control) and using the extended grip, cuts to the neck.

Secrets of the Karambit

Zombie training #4 - *(Against a right, left hook punch)*

Right inside entry and left inside entry, after cutting the left arm slice across the midsection and end with a slice to the groin using the extended grip.

Zombie training #5 - *Player 'B' hooks, 'A' blocks inside and follows with a backhand strike, but 'B' blocks it (not a grab)*

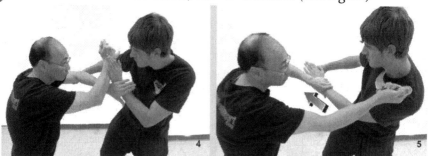

'A' reaches under to remove the obstruction, pulls the arm down and away and slices to the neck.

Secrets of the Karambit

Zombie training #6 - As 'B' hooks, 'A' blocks inside and again backhands but this time 'B' grabs the wrist...

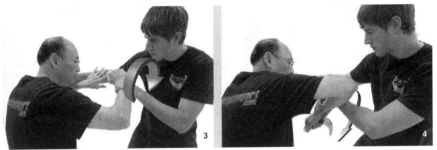

When he grabs the wrist, player 'A' lifts his elbow...

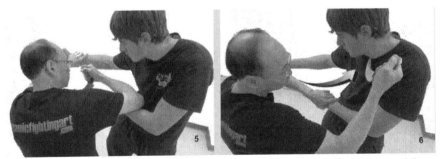

and forcefully snaps it down, breaking his grip, and finishing with a neck cut.

Next we'll show three more different ways to deal with the same grabbing technique.

Secrets of the Karambit

Empty Hand Drill #7

Zombie training #7 - As 'B' throws a hook player 'A' blocks inside and again throws a backhand strike...

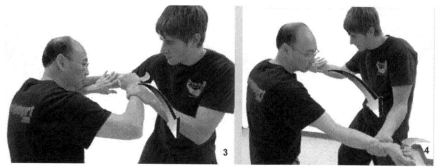

This time when 'B' grabs, player 'A' rotates his arm outward...

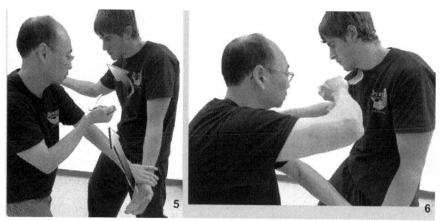

and slaps the inside of the wrist to release the grip and finish. This move is possible because 'B' is pushing outward to keep the knife away from him, the force is going out, not sideways.

176

Secrets of the Karambit

Zombie training #8 - *As 'B' throws a hook player 'A' blocks inside and again throws a backhand strike... and 'B' again grabs.*

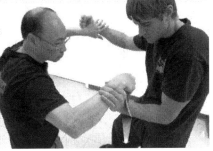

This time 'A' turns the edge of the karambit inward towards the attacker's arm and presses down, cutting into the flesh...

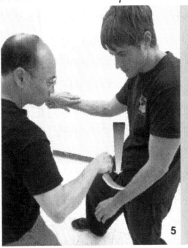
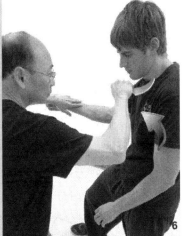

this will cause him to release his grip so that 'A' can finish the counter and escape.

Zombir training #9 - *Inside block to counter the hook and backhand strike with the karambit*

When he grabs 'A' drops his arm down and using his left hands he lifts and pulls while pushing down and forward with his right. (Remember the quick releases from chapter 13)

As he pulls the hand away he finishes with a cut to the ribs or midsection.

Chapter 21

Joint Locks

Joint locking involves manipulation of an opponent's joints in such a way as to cause pain compliance, to take them to the ground or to control the attacker by immobilizing the affected limb or joint.

This is usually done by isolating the appropriate joint and by bending, twisting or striking, you force the joint to move past its normal range of motion or move it in the opposite direction causing varying degrees of pain.

If applied forcefully and with a quick or sudden snapping motion it can cause damage to the joint, such as in muscle, tendon and ligament tears and dislocation or bone fractures.

Using the karambit to cut the attackers limb can cause him to become much more compliant and easier to manipulate into a lock. You can also use the karambit to lock and hold the assailant in position.

Joint locks can be divided into five general types depending on which section of the body they affect.

Small joint manipulation - Refers to twisting, pulling or bending fingers or toes to cause pain in the various joints of those appendages. Grabbing a finger or two is a good way for a smaller person to control or get loose from a larger attacker. If you are of a smaller frame, facing multiple attackers or a woman being attacked, don't just bend the fingers........break them. On the street an execution of this type of technique may also allow you to get to your weapon.

Wrist locks - Applied through an over-rotation of the hand and wrist-joint and possibly the distal radio ulnar articulation (a joint between the two bones in the forearm; the radius and ulna). Wrist locks are very common in most martial arts and self-defense techniques and are also widely used by law enforcement and military as pain compliance holds.

While it is generally considered to be a safe technique if applied abruptly and with force, a wrist lock can easily tear a ligament or cause dislocation of the joint.

Arm locks - An arm lock will hyper extend or over rotate the elbow and or shoulder joint causing extreme pain.

Arm locks can be used to momentarily immobilize the attacker or to take them to the ground to finish them. Arm locks such as an elbow lock or shoulder lock should not be used to try to hold them in one place or to get them to 'tap' in a street situation because they may have a friend that is standing just outside of your field of vision ready to attack you or they may resume their assault when you let them up after tapping.

Leg locks - A leg lock is directed at the ankle, knee or hip joint of the leg. These are typically not used on the street because it leaves the attacker's arms free to pull a gun or a knife from his pocket or jacket. On the street you would attack these joints using joint manipulation to off-balance or take them down.

Spinal locks - Cervical and spinal locks are applied to multiple joints in the spinal column, caused by forcing the spine beyond its normal ranges of motion, usually done by bending, cranking or twisting the head or upper body into unorthodox positions.

Spinal locks are typically either neck cranks or spine cranks and can cause severe injury to the ligaments and vertebrae similar to a whiplash, damaging the nerves which can cause a stroke or even quadriplegia.

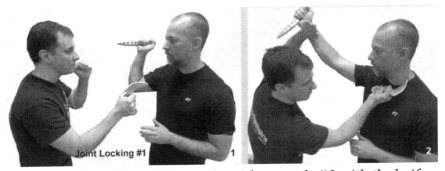

Joint Lock #1 - Player 'B' attacks with an angle #8 with the knife in the ice pick position. Player 'A' blocks and slashes the neck at the same time while using the karambit in the forward or hammer position.

Secrets of the Karambit

As 'A' blocks he immediately grabs the wrist to keep the attacker from pulling his arm back. 'A' then brings his right arm under and behind the arm and pulls back sharply into the crook of the elbow to bend the arm and allowing him to hook the wrist with the karambit.

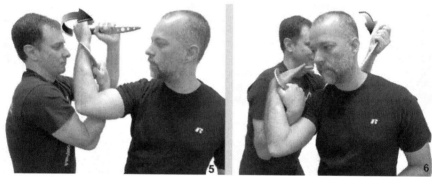

Here 'A' disarms the knife while still holding the wrist and thrusts the knife into the side of the neck.

Joint Lock #2 - The initial first three moves are the same as in Joint Lock #1

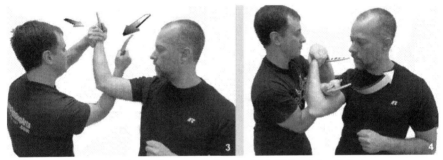

On fig. 4 after bending the arm player 'A' slides his right arm through and across the chest to hook the attacker's neck. At the same time he starts to apply pressure to the hand holding the knife by placing it against his own chest and pushing forward.

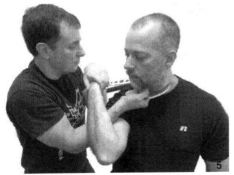

This will drive the point of the knife into the neck while hooking with the karambit from the other side.

Joint Lock #3 - *'B' attacks with a downward #8. 'A' blocks, grabs and thrusts to the midsection while twisting the hand holding the knife.*

'A' then grabs with the bottom of the hand with his right hand and continues to twist in a counter-clockwise direction.

This allows 'A' to strip the knife free as he tucks the arm into his armpit.

Secrets of the Karambit

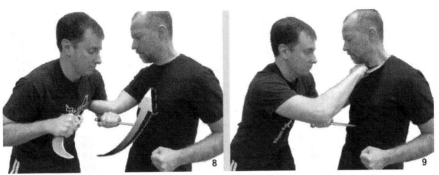

To finish he stabs to the midsection while slashing the throat.

Joint Lock #4 - *(Against an angle #1 & 2 attack)*
Player 'A' uses a split or simply leans back and slashes as the angle #1 strike goes by...

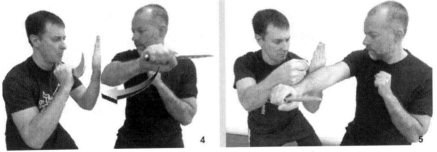

'A' then moves in for the angle #2 and blocks and cuts.

185

Secrets of the Karambit

Reaching over the top he grabs the wrist and twists while pulling with the left hand at the elbow to bend it into position

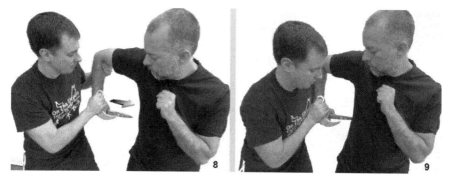

From here 'A' pushes the blade back into his attacker.

Joint Lock #5 *- (Against #1 & 2 attack) Here 'A' is using the hammer grip position.*

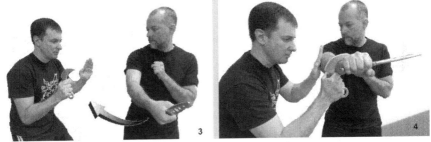

The defense is the same as the previous scenario...

Until he gets to fig. 5, from here he strips the knife by grabbing the 'gate keeper' (pad of the thumb) and pushing downward with the karambit while pulling back on his hand.

He then applies a wrist flex and digs the karambit into the crook of the elbow, pulling down and forward.

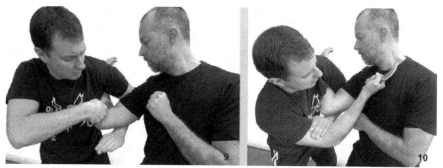

This allows him to slip the arm into a cradle joint lock and cut the neck.

Joint Lock #6 - *(Against a #1 & 2 attack)*
Player 'A' uses a split or simply leans back and slashes as the angle #1 strike goes by...

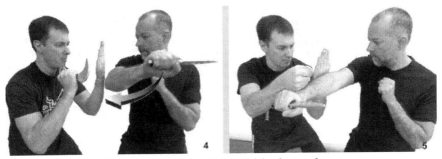

'A' then moves in for the angle #2 and blocks and cuts.

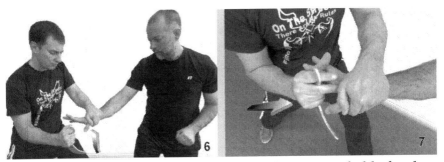

After the disarm 'A' grabs any finger that he can get ahold of and snaps it back while controlling the wrist with his left hand.

Now 'A' pulls down as he steps back, breaking the finger and bringing the attacker to the ground...

From here, it's a simple matter to cut the neck if needed.

Joint Lock #7 - *(Against #1 & 2 and adding a left hook)*
'B' evades, slices the angle #1 attack, and then blocks and disarms when the angle #2 comes back at his head.

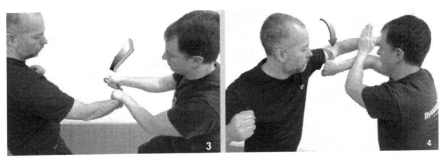

When player 'A' throws the left hook 'B' blocks and slices the biceps

Reaching over the arm 'B' scoops, grabs and cuts to the ribs.

He then brings the blade under the arm and forcefully pulls back in order the bend the arm (arm manipulation),

'B' then shoots the arm forward, slicing the neck and wraps the head, pushing down (neck manipulation)

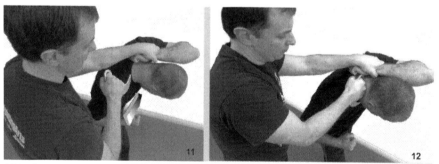

'B' then quickly steps across and cuts the neck from the other side (circular neck cut).

Joint Lock #8 - (Against angle #1 & 2 with a left hook)

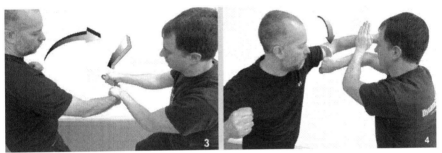

Evade, cut using a meet the force block, block the angle #2 coming back and disarm......when 'A' throws the hook punch 'B' blocks and cut the biceps...

Here he scoops, pulls the arm and slash to the ribs...

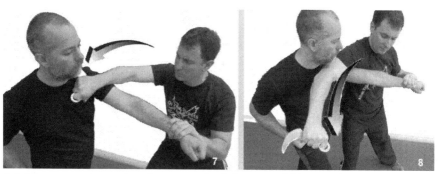

Making sure to maintain control of the arm, 'B' punches over the top of the arm catching him in the face or neck...

And continues by applying an armbar takedown and finish.

Chapter 22

Unarmed vs. Karambit

Unarmed defense against a karambit or ANY weapon is extremely difficult and actually not advised unless you have no other alternative. If you try to disarm a karambit, knife, gun, length of pipe, hammer or any weapon there is a good chance that you will be seriously injured or killed.

But there are circumstances where a loved one is being attacked or there is no doubt in your mind that the offender is going to attack to injure or kill you. With this in mind, we will present several possible scenarios.

Unarmed #1 - Slashing with an angle #1 & 2 attack - Since player 'A' doesn't have a weapon he wants to try to avoid the initial strike.

The chance for 'A' to counter is on the back swing.

Here he blocks, grabs and eye jabs to the face to temporarily blind the attacker (if you do not do something to incapacitate the attacker you will not be able to control the karambit because all of his focus will still be on attacking you with the blade)

Immediately grabbing with both hands he twists and drives the karambit back into the attacker.

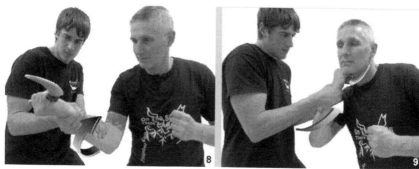

To make sure that he is finished 'A' (still controlling the arm) brings it back up to cut the throat.

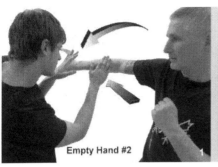 

Unarmed #2 - *As the angle #1 attack comes in player 'A' moves into middle range, blocking with both hands and thrusting out an eye jab to temporarily blind him.*

He scoops the arm using the left hand, switches grips and eye jabs again (you can substitute a punch here). Note: don't let go of his arm until you have a firm grip with the other hand.

Pull the arm back.....hard, snapping the elbow...

and apply a figure 4 lock while cutting to the neck...

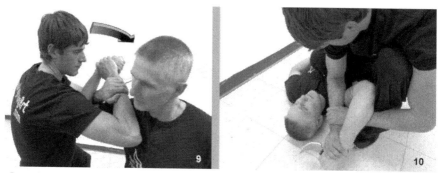

Continuing with the figure 4, sweep, taking the opponent to the ground.

Secrets of the Karambit

Unarmed #3 - *Angle #1 & 2 attack*

Player 'A' avoids the angle #1 and blocks the angle #2, while also

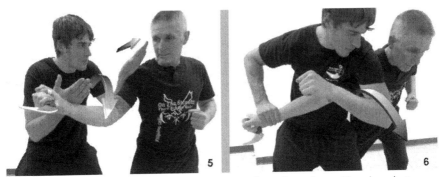

using an eye jab, grabbing the weapons hand and continuing into a standing armbar.

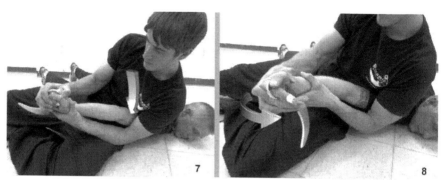

He sweeps him to the ground, controls the arm...

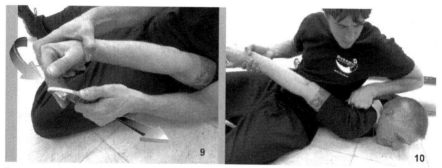

by twisting or bending the wrist he is able to dislodge the karambit to finish the attacker.

Chapter 23

Karambit vs. Straight Blade

Being confronted with a knife is always scary and always dangerous, but if it does happen there are a few things to remember:

Stay calm by breathing deeply you can also try clenching and unclenching your hands so that you don't 'freeze' up.

Watch the criminals shoulders or chest, by looking in this area you can use your peripheral vision to monitor the arms and hands. When the attack starts, the shoulders will move first.

You don't want to stare them in the eyes because they may be an extremely cold, cruel and terrifying looking person, and this could intimidate you into inaction. In addition, if you are staring at their eyes and then quickly start looking around, your eyes may give away your intention to attempt something.

Same thing with the weapon, the more that you stare at it the more frightening and 'larger' it becomes.

Knife attacks are not like in the movies and not like what you practice in self-defense class. No one will execute one thrust towards your mid-section and then stop and 'pose' for you while you execute your technique.

In a knife fight there are no winners, everyone gets cut or stabbed. What we are discussing is trying to alleviate the immediate threat so that we can make our escape.

The following are a few examples:

Knife #1 - Here player 'A' avoids and slashes on the initial attack

He moves into middle range and blocks it on the return strike

Here 'A' executes a knife disarm...

But before 'A' can finish the counter his attacker grabs 'A's wrist.

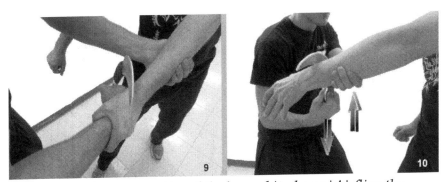

Using the unique properties of the karambit player 'A' flips the karambit up to position it over the wrist. He then pulls the arm up with his left hand while pulling down with his right.

Secrets of the Karambit

Knife #2 - *Inside entry to block the strike and then....*

Scoop, cut and disarm the knife.

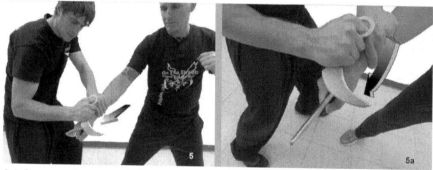

Make sure to control the 'gatekeeper' (pad of the thumb) by squeezing to loosen his grip as you push the blade out of his hand.

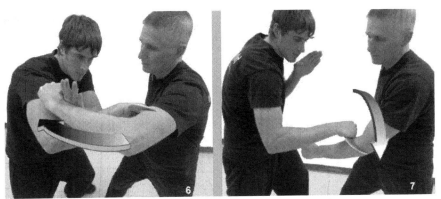

'B' throws a left hook which 'A' blocks and scoops the arm...

'A' then grabs with the left and using the edge of the karambit executes an inside arm drag...

pulling his head forward and into his blade.

Secrets of the Karambit

Knife #3 - Inside entry to block the attack...

scoop and cut...

disarm the knife...

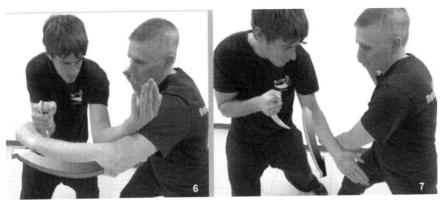

'B' throws a left hook which 'A' blocks and scoops with his left hand and...

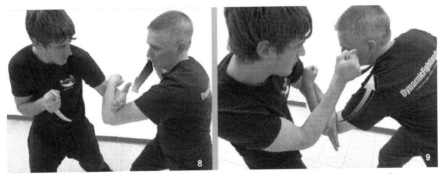

continuing the scooping motion, 'A' applies an arm drag and cuts.

Secrets of the Karambit

Knife #4 - Inside block,

cut up and scoop the arm...

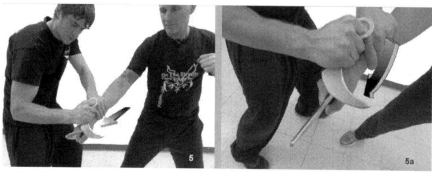

as he disarms, 'B' throws a left hook...

208

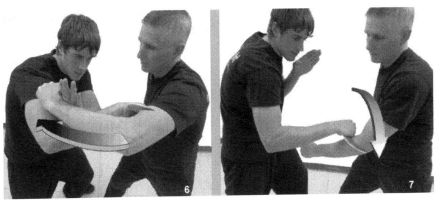

block the hook, cut and scoop using the karambit...

grab the wrist, scoop the right arm under and pull back, causing the arm to bend...

shoot the knife through and cut to the neck.

Knife #5 - *Block the angle #1 attack, cut*

and scoop, but this time grab the hand at the pad of the thumb (gate keeper) with the left hand...

and 'A' applies a wrist flex, for the disarm 'A' inserts the karambit at the bottom of the handle to disarm it from the bottom.

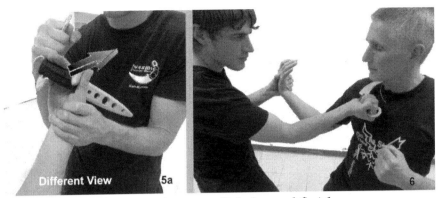

Push the karambit up and over to dislodge and finish.

Knife #6 - Inside block and scoop,

grab the hand holding the weapon and apply a wrist flex...

From here 'A' employs a quick cut to the wrist and then turns the hand over,

This allows 'A' to disarm the knife and finish. (He could also have skipped the disarm and gone straight to the throat after cutting the wrist).

Knife #7 - *This time player 'A' uses a downward cut, this allows him to easily pass the arm overhead*

Where he catches it with his left hand and disarms

Following the disarm, he cuts into the crook of the elbow (manipulation) causing 'B' to lift his arm to try to get away from the knife.

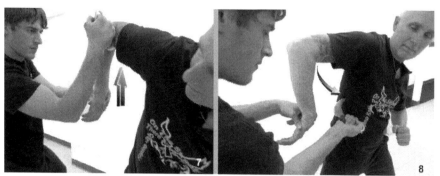

'A' keeps the pressure on the wrist to hold the arm in position until he can follow up with a cut to the ribs.

Knife #8 - *Following a split entry off of an angle #1 attack.*

Player 'A' moves in with a quick motion while controlling the arm and cuts the neck.

Secrets of the Karambit

Knife #9 - *(Against a #1 & #4 attack)*
Player 'A' uses a split entry to evade the initial strike...

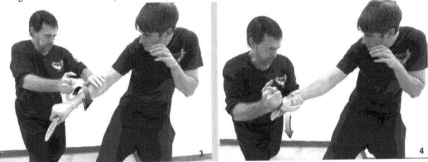

while cutting the arm on the backswing and disarming the knife.

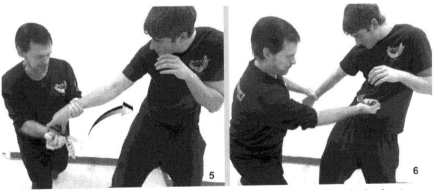

By maintaining the grip and twisting the weapons hand clockwise, he opens him up for a slash to the mid-section.

The next three techniques were shown in the Empty Hand training portion (Zombie Apocalypse), this is what they would look like against a blade.

Knife #10 - *(Against a #1 & #2 attack)*
Player 'A' attacks with an angle #1, 'B' uses a split entry to avoid and cut his arm.

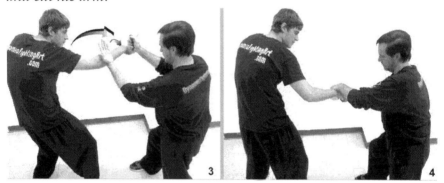

When 'A' comes back with an angle #4 'B' blocks, cuts and disarms.

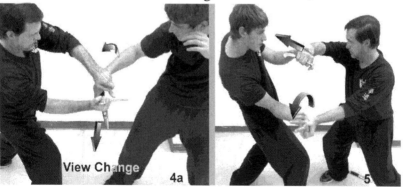

(Note: disarm shown from the other view for clarity) *Disarm and apply a wrist flex with the left hand.*

'B' then throws a backhand strike to the neck which is caught by player 'A'. 'B' quickly raises his elbow and forcefully snaps it downward with a quick jerking motion.

 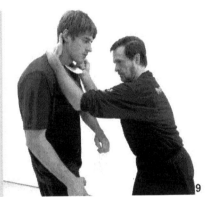

This should result in bringing his head forward and if you notice when you snap your elbow down it will also move your blade right into position for the next cut. Grab the back of the neck with your left hand and step on his front foot so that he can't move away.

Knife #11 - *(Against a #1 & #2 attack)*
Player 'A' attacks with an angle #1, 'B' uses a split entry to avoid and cut his arm

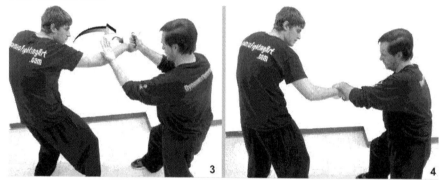

When 'A' comes back with an angle #4 'B' blocks, cuts and disarms.

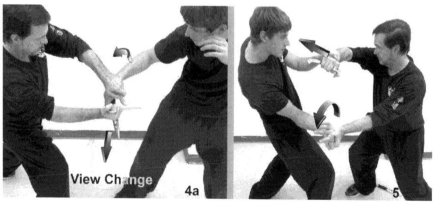

(Note: disarm shown from the other view for clarity) Disarm and apply a wrist flex with the left hand. 'B' then throws a backhand strike to the neck which is caught by player 'A'.

'B' then rotates the arm to the right 45-90 deg. This is possible because the attacker's force is coming forward, towards player 'B' not side to side.

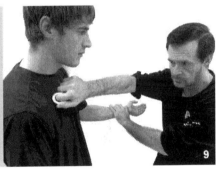

Slap forcefully on the wrist to dislodge his grip and finish.

Knife #12 - *(Against a #1 & #2 attack)*
Player 'A' attacks with an angle #1, 'B' uses a split entry to avoid and cuts his attackers arm.

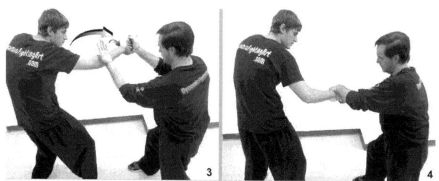

When 'A' comes back with an angle #4 'B' blocks, cuts and disarms.

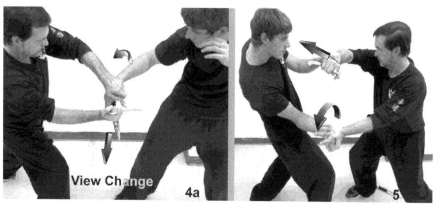

(Note: disarm shown from the other view for clarity) Disarm and apply a wrist flex with the left hand.

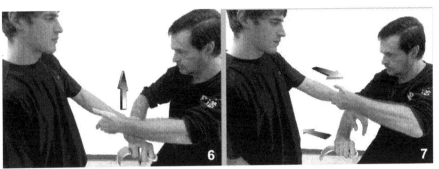

Here 'B' drops his arm straight down and releasing the wrist flex he lifts with the left hand, pulling his arm free...

and finish with a cut to the midsection.

Knife #13 - *(Against a #1 & #2 attack)*
Player 'A' attacks with an angle #1, 'B' uses a split entry to avoid and cuts his attackers arm.

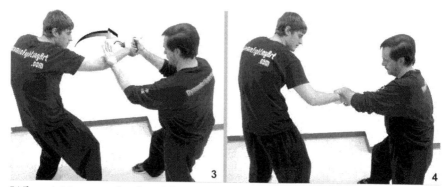

When 'A' comes back with an angle #4 'B' blocks, cuts and disarms.

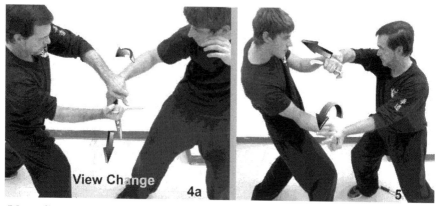

(Note: disarm shown from the other view for clarity) Disarm and apply a wrist flex with the left hand.

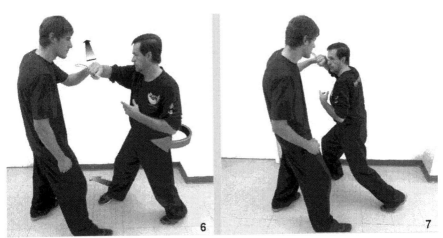

'B' takes a big step at a 45 degree angle and at the same time pulls his arm back in order to deliver a punch to the face with the karambit. (you can release the wrist flex if needed)

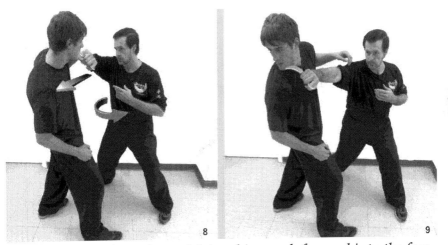

Here 'B' twists the waist and drives his punch forward into the face or neck. The punching motion will break the opponent's grip on his wrist.

Angle #5 - Thrust

Knife #14 - *(Against a thrusting attack)*
Player 'B' attacks with an angle #5 thrust, 'A' blocks down with his left hand to guide the knife away from his body and simultaneously cuts the neck.

'A' then scoops the arm to move it away from his body and...

stepping in while still controlling the weapon hand finishes with a cut to the ribs.

Secrets of the Karambit

Knife #15 - *(Against a thrusting attack)*
Player 'B' attacks with an angle #5 thrust, 'A' parries to the right with his left hand to guide the knife away from his body and simultaneously cuts the biceps...

'A' then flips the karambit to the extended grip...

and steps inside to finish with a supported neck cut.

NOTES

Chapter 24

Karambit vs. Gun

Being threatened with a gun is a worst case scenario and if the attacker only wants your valuables then the safest option is to give it to them. The only time that you should try to fight back against a gun is when there is no other option and you know that your life is in danger, for example, if they just shot your companion and now they are turning the gun at you or if they want you to go to another location with them.

Remember, once you get into a car with them, your chances of being found alive are not very good.

Be aware that in order for a gun defense to work you MUST be close enough to touch them without having to step or run towards them, you cannot step as fast as their finger can pull the trigger. If you do decide to act you must attack hard, fast and aggressively, because you will not get another chance.

If you do try to grab the weapon or strike the assailant, there are some things to watch for:

If their grip is too tight on the gun you may not be able to wrest it from them.

If you are not fast enough or firm enough with your grab or attack, they will just step back and pull the gun away from you.

They may punch you with their other hand.

Even if you get the weapon they will move towards you to try to retrieve it so you must be prepared to shoot.

On the other hand, you may have a conceal carry license and possess a gun of your own which you keep on your person.

Now this is a great deterrent and will give you a better option to fight back and protect yourself and your family, but what if you can't get to your gun? What if they get the drop on you, catch you by surprise or suddenly grab you. What if you are in an area where guns are not allowed? What do you do then? This is where your empty hand skills and better yet your karambit can come into play.

You may be able to counter attack with your karambit until you can get to your gun. If grabbed perhaps you can cut yourself free, allowing you to get to your firearm. All the firearms training in the world won't help you if you can't get your weapon out of the holster and be able to engage the threat.

You never know what type of a situation you will be in and while a gun is a great equalizer at a distance, a karambit works as well if not better when up close and personal.

Secrets of the Karambit

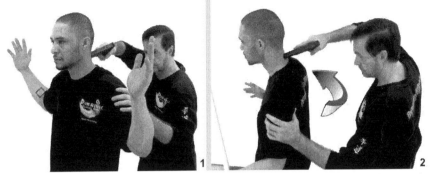

Gun scenario #1 - *The attacker comes up from behind and demands cash.*

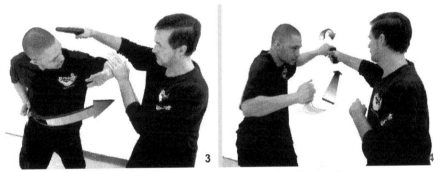

As 'A' is reaching for his 'wallet' he grabs his karambit, spins, grabbing the gun hand and moving it off-line...

Slashes to the arm to disarm the attacker and then to the throat. Note: Do not let go of the hand holding the gun until the threat is stopped.

Gun scenario #2 - *The attacker confronts player 'A' from the front. 'A' moves his hands up to a non-threatening position. Here he moves off-line, grabs the gun and pulls the karambit in one smooth motion.*

Maintaining control of the gun 'A' quickly slashes to the throat.

Final Thoughts

The karambit has been around for thousands of years and has recently been 'discovered' by the western world over the past few decades.

When using it on the job it is an abundantly versatile utility tool to have and it has a variety of useful functions. For protection remember to keep it simple, don't try any fancy techniques or manipulations because under times of stress your fine motor skills will be limited.

Remember also that it is important to practice with your karambit, and to always use a training blade and safety glasses when working with a partner.

It is also best to get some personal instruction by book, video or professional trainer and practice, practice, practice, there's nothing worse than not being able to get to your karambit when you need it or cutting yourself with your own knife.

I hope that you have enjoyed this book and that you have found it helpful, whether you are interested in the karambit for martial arts, recreation, something work related or personal defense.

NOTES

APPENDICES

To view video clips of some of the preceding drills and techniques shown in this book go to:

https://goo.gl/YEuuQR

NOTES

ADDITIONAL READING

Karambit: Exotic Weapon of the Indonesian Archipelago
by Steve Tarani

Mastering the Curved Blade
by Steve Tarani

Filipino Martial Culture (Martial Culture Series)
by Mark V. Wiley

Filipino Combat Systems:
An Introduction to An Ancient Art For Modern Times
by Mark Edward Cody & Ray Dionaldi

KunTao - The esoteric martial art of Southeast Asia
by David Seiwert

The Weapons & Fighting Arts of Indonesia
by Donn F. Draeger

The Malay Art of Self-Defense
by Sheikh Shamsuddin

The Filipino Martial Arts
by Dan Inosanto, Gilbert Johnson & George Foon

REFERENCES

https://en.wikipedia.org/wiki/Java

https://en.wikipedia.org/wiki/Nunchaku

https://en.wikipedia.org/wiki/Minangkabau_people

https://en.wikipedia.org/wiki/Ethnic_Malays

https://en.wikipedia.org/wiki/Kalis

https://en.wikipedia.org/wiki/Kris

https://en.wikipedia.org/wiki/Steel

http://www.prayway.com/unreached/clusters/8045.html

https://en.wikipedia.org/wiki/Janbiya

https://commons.wikimedia.org/wiki/File:Jambiya.jpg#/media/File:Jambiya.jpg

https://commons.wikimedia.org/wiki/File:Ottoman_jambiya.jpg#/media/File:Ottoman_jambiya.jpg

https://commons.wikimedia.org/wiki/File:Jambiya_from_Yemen.jpg#/media/File:Jambiya_from_Yemen.jpg

http://www.academia.edu/6441820/The_Yemeni_Janbiya_and_its_various_parts

http://sharpeningmadeeasy.com/steels.htm

http://www.stormthecastle.com/blacksmithing/blacksmithing-a-knife/steels-and-metals-for-knifemaking-and-knifesmithing.htm

http://www.osograndeknives.com/catalog/blade-steels.html

http://www.historyworld.net/wrldhis/PlainTextHistories.asp?gtrack=pthc&ParagraphID=ahh#ahh#ixzz3vgCbkH8Q

http://www.nytimes.com/1981/09/29/science/the-mystery-of-damascus-steel-appears-solved.html

http://metalsupermarkets.com/blog/types-of-steel/

http://metals.about.com/od/properties/a/Steel-Types-And-Properties.htm

http://www.worldsteel.org/Steel-facts.html

http://www.bladehq.com/cat--Steel-Types--332

https://youtu.be/6LHmsinNM6s (making damascas steel - hand forge)

http://www.karambit.com

http://www.karambit.com/about-steve-tarani/

http://stevetarani.com

https://en.wikipedia.org/wiki/Karambit

https://en.wikipedia.org/wiki/Gravity_knife

https://www.knife-depot.com/learn/best-survival-knife

https://www.knife-depot.com/knife-information-160.html

https://www.krudoknives.com/krudo-khronicles/knife-deployment-101

https://en.wikipedia.org/wiki/Switchblade

https://www.knife-depot.com/blog/a-guide-to-the-types-of-knife-locking-systems

http://coolmaterial.com/roundup/the-history-of-the-pocket-knife/

https://en.wikipedia.org/wiki/Pocketknife

www.japaneseswordindex.com

http://www.aoijapan.com/

http://www.everydaycommentary.com/2013/01/edc-primer-deployment-methods-or-why.html

http://lifehacker.com/5890207/give-your-folding-knife-assisted-opening-capabilities-with-zip-ties

http://www.personaldefensenetwork.com/article/optimizing-the-everyday-carry-folding-knife-for-personal-protection/

http://www.offthegridnews.com/self-defense/knives-101-when-you-must-carry-a-blade-instead-of-a-gun-for-self-defense/

http://www.osograndeknives.com/catalog/blade-steels.html

http://talonknife.com/carrying-a-neck-knife/

http://americanconcealed.com/three-ways-your-body-goes-crazy-during-a-violent-attack/

http://americanconcealed.com/how-to-stay-calm-in-combat/

http://www.yourhormones.info/Hormones/Adrenaline.aspx

https://en.wikipedia.org/wiki/Tueller_Drill

http://www.ncbi.nlm.nih.gov/pubmed/23849364

http://www.policemag.com/channel/weapons/articles/2015/09/instinct-and-knife-attack-defense.aspx

http://www.guillaumeerard.com/aikido/articles/defense-against-a-knife-attack-the-principles-of-an-efficient-response

http://www.hilaryking.net/glossary/startle-response.html

http://www.effective-mind-control.com/startle-response.html

https://web.archive.org/web/20090220063137/http://tipunan.com/Publications/martial_arts/harimaw-buno.html

https://en.wikipedia.org/wiki/Dumog

http://www.warriorseskrima.com/wp-content/uploads/2011/02/Grapplingeskrima.pdf

www.krishnagodhania.org

https://en.wikipedia.org/wiki/Joint_lock

http://www.clearwaterkungfu.com/our-curriculum/qin-na/

http://pacificwavejiujitsu.com/blog/how-joint-locks-work-in-the-martial-arts/

https://en.wikipedia.org/wiki/Spinal_lock

https://en.wikipedia.org/wiki/Armlock

http://www.womenshealthmag.com/life/self-defense-techniques

http://attackproof.com/i-m-a-woman-needing-self-defense-training.html

http://www.womensselfdefense-seps.com/womensselfdefense-selfdefense.html

http://pistolcombatives.com/2013/07/14/practice-deploying-your-firearm/

http://www.functionalselfdefense.org/weapons/gun-threat-defense

http://www.aware.org/self-defense/is-important

http://jawaraweaponshop.blogspot.com/

http://www.journalofasianmartialarts.com/category/other-areas/indonesia-list-products-46

https://www.facebook.com/pages/cimpago-photography/108030565945485

http://gemintang.com/dunia-film-musik/seni-bela-diri-asli-indonesia/

NOTES

About the Author

David Seiwert has been studying, teaching and training in a wide range of martial arts from Japan, Korea, China, Thailand, Indonesia and the Philippines since the age of 12 years.

He is currently semi-retired from the engineering field and regularly travels to Southeast Asia to further increase his knowledge and understanding of these indigenous arts.

When not traveling he spends his time teaching, giving seminars, writing books and producing videos about the fighting systems of these regions.

For more information or training material on the martial arts, he can be contacted at:

www.DavidSeiwert.com
www.DynamicFightingArt.com
www.DfaMediaProductions.com

Made in the USA
Columbia, SC
21 February 2019